BRAIN
GAIN

BRAIN GAIN

Timely Tools to Tackle
Life's Heavy Lifting

LAURIE LEITCH, PhD

LIONCREST

PUBLISHING

Brain Gain

Timely Tools to Tackle Life's Heavy Lifting

ISBN 978-1-5445-4000-9 Paperback
      978-1-5445-4001-6 Ebook
      978-1-5445-4002-3 Audiobook

FIRST EDITION

Disclaimer

The contents of this book are not intended for medical use or as a substitute for psychotherapy.

CONTENTS

INTRODUCTION

How This Book Is Different from Other Self-Help Books

Have you ever tried a self-help book that didn't work for you? Many of them leave out the most important fundamental factors and focus primarily on the cognitive level—on thinking and how your thoughts trip you up. But that's only a symptom of the problem, just an indicator of something even more basic than thinking. Other books focus on the emotional level, on feelings—again, a symptom but not the heart of the matter.

This book is different from other self-help books, focusing on the foundation of all human functioning: your brain and nervous system.

Your nervous system includes your brain and the many pathways of nerves all over your body that receive information from your body's cells and the outside world. Neuroscience gives us a map of how this complex system operates. This book applies neuroscience to provide you with essential building blocks for success in achieving and maintaining overall health and well-being—a healthy body, peak job performance, and robust relationships.

This book will specifically show you the miraculous process in our brains called neuroplasticity, which is our brain's ability to grow and change…in both good and not-so-good ways. In the various communities I work in, people get very excited to know they have the power to make their own brains better.

Every one of us is born with the capacity to be resilient, but many events happen over the years to deplete resilience. This book provides practical information on how to build it back up. You can probably list several events that have taken away some of your resilience. And as a result, you might experience a negative impact on your health, relationship challenges, job problems, and maybe even a diminished quality of life in general. But you don't have to be a captive of your history. Don't stay stuck in current patterns that, at best, prevent you from getting to where you want to be, and at worst, get you nowhere at all.

This book offers you a program—the Brain Gain Program (BGP)—that can give your natural resilience a huge boost. Because the program uses building blocks that are based in neuroscience, once you learn to make the changes you want, you will also know how to make them stick. Exciting, too, is that, after you learn the program for your own self-care, this book invites you to introduce the BGP to the groups that matter to you. You can choose to be a Resilience Messenger!

You'll learn exactly how to be a messenger for resilience in your church, school, or community—a step-by-step way to become a Resilience Messenger, including a special tool, the BGP Skills Card, which you can use for yourself and to share the program with others, even kids.

Yes, it is so simple that even a young child can learn to use it. I've taught the skills in many kinds of communities, to kids as young as four and adults in their eighties, and even to men and women in prison, including genocide perpetrators in Rwanda.

Are you ready to create the self you want to be by simply paying attention to sensory cues from your body? Let's go!

Chapter 1

THE REAL DEAL ABOUT RESILIENCE

The word "resilience" has become so frequently used that I almost didn't use it in this book. But it is exactly the right word for what can help you change your life for the better: better physical and emotional health, better relationships with family and friends, and better success at work. You're entitled to that!

The common meaning of resilience is "the ability to bounce back." But I prefer this definition: "the ability to move forward and be generative after challenges." The latter goes beyond bouncing back to bouncing *forward*. Doesn't that sound better?

A PROFOUND STORY
OF RESILIENCE

A story from my work in Kenya illustrates this second form of resilience. It starts in a camp for displaced persons, about a three-hour drive from Nairobi. People who didn't have enough to eat or drink, covered with the dust of parched, inhospitable earth, filled the camp.

A human rights organization asked me to go to this part of Kenya after a government election that spawned a lot of postelection violence. Government officials worried that more people would be badly injured if they remained in their villages. In an effort to stop the violence, which included horrible machete injuries and deaths, the government paid a small sum of money to any villager who agreed to relocate to one of several large tented camps for displaced people.

I had been doing this practical neuroscience-based work nationally (in the US) and internationally for many years; I worked with the villagers in these camps to help them process the fear and trauma they were experiencing as a result of the violence. My team worked in three camps. The first two were in big, flat, dusty fields of nothingness. Nothing grew—no trees for shade, no grass. There was nothing except a hundred or so tents. And there was nothing for anyone to do—no playgrounds for kids or exercise areas for adults. People just wandered around, waiting for the water truck and food delivery. Life in these camps was extremely bleak.

But the third camp was strikingly different. Every tent had a green garden growing out of the dust. Hoses were connected to a water truck, and some of that water was used to create vegetable gardens. The camp also had a large school tent and smaller tents where microfinance projects—projects that enabled individuals and groups to develop work that paid them—took place. This included the sale of beautiful handwoven baskets. I bought one to bring home.

I was startled at the difference in this third camp and asked my local contact why it was so different. She told me that the government had paid each villager (for all three camps) the same small fee to persuade them to relocate. In the first two camps, the people took the money and held onto it, but in the third camp, they pooled their money, and with that much larger sum they purchased the land the camp was on.

Their ownership of the land motivated them to plan for the future—to plant gardens, make and sell baskets, and get involved in other microfinance projects. They had formed a governing structure to foster group decision-making. They were selling baskets and vegetables to buy a bus to take the children to school and transport women to the hospital to safely birth their babies.

Are you wondering what the kind of resilience I'm describing in the story about Kenya has to do with you? I'll tell you. We know from neuroscience—the scientific study of what the brain requires to do its very best—that when people respond with fear to life's challenges, it affects their health, their relationships, and even their capacity to think clearly.

The people in the first two camps were making fear-based decisions. They didn't trust one another, had very little hope, and felt dependent on government officials for their physical and financial security. Conversely, in camp three, a small group of people had come together, determined to create something better for the entire community.

First, they met to generate a bunch of ideas. Then they reached out to others in the community to get them interested in joining the efforts. As word spread throughout the camp that some exciting plans were being discussed, more and more people wanted to be part of the partnership effort. Instead of fear, they felt excitement and determination. This is a beautiful example of resilience—bouncing forward—as well as the power of shared purpose and relationships to diminish fear and despair.

THE POWER OF PARTNERING

The contents of this book will equip you with a potent, science-based program to consistently improve your life for the long term in ways that are important to you. But I am also proposing a very thrilling partnership in that you can become a Resilience Messenger to take the neuroscience-based information to your community, so the circle of resilience widens, like those in the successful camp in Kenya did.

You have a lot of control over your brain and nervous system. It's a superpower! You don't have to be stuck in negative patterns. You don't have to be a pessimist or a hothead or insecure. You can build a brain that serves your best interests. I've never understood why, but very few people know about this ability to change the brain. Such an important piece of personal power should be taught starting in preschool.

Most of us have never learned how hugely important the body's signals are to who you become as a person. You'll learn to notice when you feel calm, relaxed, or energized. And you'll learn to track agitation, a pounding heart, or a shutting down. But most essentially, you'll learn exactly what to do about these responses when you notice them.

You can find out what's happening in your brain and nervous system by noticing sensations in your body. This provides direct guidance to change what isn't working well. You'll be able to manage challenging emotions such as reactivity, anger, or hopelessness. This is also a very exciting way to intensify the positives in your life. This kind of *noticing* is called "Sensory Tracking"; it's one of the BGP skills, and it can change all aspects of your life for the better!

ALL HUMANS START WITH THE SAME BASIC BRAIN

All of us, wherever we live in the world, have the same structures and processes in our brains. What makes each of us different is the ways the brain changes based on experiences. This includes factors such as quality of nutrition, emotional support, and growth opportunities like education. People can apply the BGP, using the skills in this book, to take charge of their life's trajectory in amazing ways:

1. building the brain that works for them in order to be the best they can be
2. cutting off poisonous stress chemicals, which cause major illnesses and create multigenerational health problems in oppressed groups
3. thinking strategically in problem-solving situations, and
4. building healthy and nourishing relationships.

The BGP has been taught to people of color who live daily with the impact of systemic racism, military veterans hospitalized with chronic pain and PTSD, prisoners and formerly incarcerated citizens, healthcare providers in medical settings, and first responders after natural disasters. It is taught to average folks who have a strong desire to be the best they can be.

You have a lot of control over what you "wire" into your brain. That's what makes you who you are and who you want to be as an individual. I invite you to partner with me in this work, first to learn BGP for yourself and then to become a Resilience Messenger by taking the BGP into your community. I hope you'll join me in this partnership!

THE QUESTION THAT GRABBED MY ATTENTION

Have you ever been asked a question that shakes your foundation and motivates you to take action? I had such an experience. Someone once asked me this challenging question: "Do you think that teaching the BGP to people who have lived with the effects of discrimination, systemic racism, and other forms of oppression in order to decrease reactivity and maintain steadiness and balance could make them complacent about the ways oppression continues to affect their lives?"

I was horrified to think this could be true. We live in a world full of injustice and oppression. The terrible impact of this oppression is reflected in a wide range of consequences for marginalized communities.

I thought long and hard about the values my program is based on and the goals of the program. I asked people who live daily with oppression but have learned the BGP—some who even teach the program—what they thought about that question. I found that they believed the program positively affected their quality of life and dignity.

Chapter 2

WHAT DOES DIGNITY HAVE TO DO WITH IT?

Have you ever felt like there are people in some groups who have important information that others don't? The most relevant occurrence of this, for the purposes of this book, is the fact that, in general, only very well-educated people tend to have learned about neuroscience, the science about how the brain works, grows, and changes, and the ways to use the information in practical and effective ways. We're going to change that!

I witnessed this firsthand when I visited a government agency to meet with a commissioner in charge of a very large service delivery system. She wanted to explore the prospect of offering my training in the BGP to her staff and the communities they serve.

After a few minutes of describing the neuroscience that is at the foundation of my program, she stopped me with a comment that really stunned me. She said, "A lot of those words seem like jargon. Why do *they* need to know those words?"

DIGNITY DEPRIVATION

I was stunned at her tone of voice, particularly how she said "they" when referring to her community members. She almost sneered when she said it. In that moment, I realized I was face-to-face with the elitism that can characterize some of our care systems. She meant that as long as the people in charge have the information needed to take care of vulnerable people, the people themselves ("they") don't need to know the information. They only have to follow the instructions of the ones who do know. This is a form of dignity deprivation.

Elitism tends to show up when some groups have important information others don't, even when it is information that is easily understood and used by anyone. The science of how the brain works, grows, and changes can benefit many people, especially when they learn practical skills to make the best use of the information. I am grateful to that commissioner for exposing elitist attitudes that, unfortunately, are commonly held.

That day, I vowed to take my program directly to the people who need it and equip them with knowledge, including accurate neuroscientific terms about the brain and nervous system, as well as the relevant skills needed to live purposeful, passionate, and meaningful lives.

You may have experienced someone talking down to you when you have gone to them for some type of help or service. Or, perhaps a staffer at an agency, store, or organization has acted like you were invisible or treated you like you were suspicious. Did it make you mad or sad? Or did you go into shutdown mode?

A silent elitism pervades many organizations we must interact with to get things done in our lives, including staying healthy. There is some very good news—it doesn't have to be like that, and we're going to change it!

There is dignity in having access to information and skills that allow you to take charge of your own mental and physical health. World Health Organization leaders call it "health literacy." With the information in this book, you will be able to actually build the brain you want, learning to interrupt stressful experiences before the toxic chemicals begin to flow in your brain and body. This is health literacy in action.

The neuroscience-based information I provide, along with the skills this book outlines, can help you increase your personal power, amplify your ability to stay cool under stress, build satisfying relationships, and be your own best advocate. First, let's explore some facts about your amazing brain.

TRY THE SIEGEL HAND BRAIN MODEL

Hold up your hand with all five fingers stretched upward, and fold your thumb into the palm of that hand. Next, fold your four outstretched fingers over your thumb. Brain scientist Dan Siegel calls this "the hand model of the brain" to illustrate the brain's three major parts—the brain stem, limbic system, and cortex.

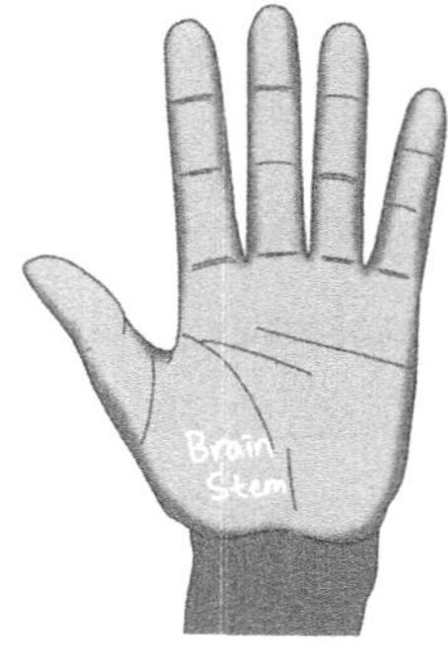

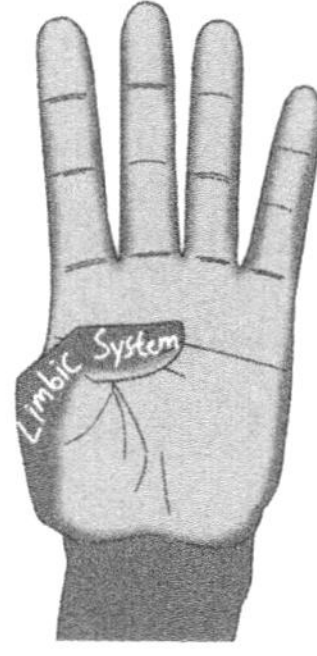

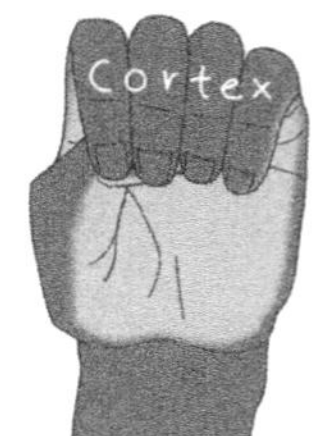

Brain Stem

The palm of your hand at the top of your wrist represents the brain stem. That's the part of the brain that controls all bodily responses that happen automatically, like breathing (kind of important, right?), eye blinking, digestion, and the three unconscious defensive responses of fight, flight, and freeze.

Your brain stem also processes information that comes into the body from your five senses (actually, there are many more than five senses) and sends it farther up the brain, where it is translated into emotions, actions, and thoughts.

Limbic System

Your thumb represents the middle part of your brain—the limbic system, which focuses on processing and regulating your emotions. It also manages short-term memory storage and retrieval, two functions essential to the way you learn. We'll focus a lot more on that part of your brain.

Cortex

The four fingers that cover your thumb like a fist represent the cortex, which is considered the thinking part of your brain. The elaborate cortex of humans allows us to think in complex ways, setting us apart from other animals. But this part of the brain can get really scrambled during stress so that you have difficulty thinking clearly and can become very reactive in troublesome ways.

STRESS AND YOUR CORTEX

Think about a time when you were running very late for an important event. As stress chemicals begin building and flooding your brain, you may notice mishaps such as misplacing your keys or phone. You might not be able to think strategically since stress chemicals block clear thinking. You may lash out at others or make bad decisions when stress chemicals affect your cortex. Stress chemicals detract from you being your best self. And stress chemicals also poison your body.

Now, lift your "cortex" up a little—raise those four fingers—so you can see your thumb again. Your thumb represents the middle part of your brain, the limbic system, which is responsible for your emotions. When people are in emotional distress, they often "flip their lids." Go ahead and flip your lid by quickly raising those four fingers. This represents what happens to clear thinking under stress. It goes offline. You might make bad decisions, make statements you wish you hadn't, or go into shutdown and seem to be emotionless.

Can you think of an example from your life when you flipped out to the extreme? Can you think of a time when someone else flipped their lid in a way that was painful for you? We also call this "reactivity." When you flip your lid, clear thinking disappears. Relationships can be harmed when you flip your lid. The good news is that you're going to learn how to manage that kind of reactivity.

CHILDREN'S BRAINS UNDER STRESS

We now know from brain imaging that the hippocampus, a particular brain structure in the limbic system, can actually shrink in size in some children who have experienced traumatic events in their young lives. Since the hippocampus is where short-term memory is stored in the brain, just think about what that means. That child won't be able to as effectively store and remember information learned in school. The child may struggle with tests, forget assignments, or lose sight of a teacher's expectations.

REACTIVITY
AND PHYSICAL HEALTH

We know reactive behavior exacerbates relationship problems, but another major concern of stress and reactivity is how they influence physical health. Several years ago, I was working in a maximum-security prison for men, teaching the BGP. When I asked the men how many had gotten into trouble because of reactivity, every single one raised a hand. Then I asked if they or anyone in their family had suffered from heart disease, and almost every hand went up. When I asked about other common stress-related illnesses, including cancer, asthma, and diabetes, again, nearly every hand was raised. Reactivity, stress, and illness go hand in hand, and many chronic health problems are seen in one generation after another.

Stress causes inflammatory processes. This is important to know, not only because stress can cause all kinds of problematic behaviors but also because stress causes inflammation in the body. Every chronic illness, such as cancer or heart disease, starts with an inflammatory process. In the following chapters, you will learn to interrupt stressors and deepen your resilience, so small stressors don't influence you to become reactive rather than responsive.

Chapter 3

THE AMYGDALA IS YOUR BRAIN'S SMOKE DETECTOR

Do you have a smoke detector in your home? It's a very important tool to signal a fire, giving you time to call the fire department, pour water on whatever is burning, or quickly get out of the house. But sometimes, smoke detectors malfunction. They're triggered just from the steam of a teakettle or if your toast starts to burn in the toaster. This is dangerous because you might just ignore that smoke detector if it goes off when there really is smoke or fire.

YOUR BRAIN
HAS A SMOKE DETECTOR

Each of us has a pair of smoke detectors, amygdalae, in the limbic system or middle part of the brain. There is one amygdala in each half, or hemisphere, of the brain. These two internal detectors are designed as a way for your brain to monitor signals of novelty, threat, or danger in your environment. But, like smoke detectors, sometimes they make mistakes about what is or isn't a threat. This can cause a big mess for you.

Here's an example. Justin has a history of being abused as a child. Because of that series of traumatic events, he grew up unable to trust anyone. Whenever someone is nice to him, he gets panicky. His heart pounds, his stomach aches, and his thinking gets foggy. As a result, he doesn't let anyone get emotionally close to him.

Another way to say this is that his amygdala is miscalibrated. It perceives everyone as a threat to him even when they aren't. The amygdala sends warning signals throughout his nervous system that create fear and reactivity. In his fear, Justin pushes everyone away. He's a lonely guy. The good news is that this miscalibration is fixable.

YOUR AMYGDALA
AND THREAT

Ready to get acquainted with your brain's smoke detector? Learning about your tiny-but-powerful amygdala will help you make sense of your own reactivity and how to manage it. Remember Dan Siegel's "hand brain" from Chapter 2? Open your hand again and put your thumb across your palm. See your thumbnail? That's your amygdala. Open both hands like that, and those thumbnails are your amygdalae.

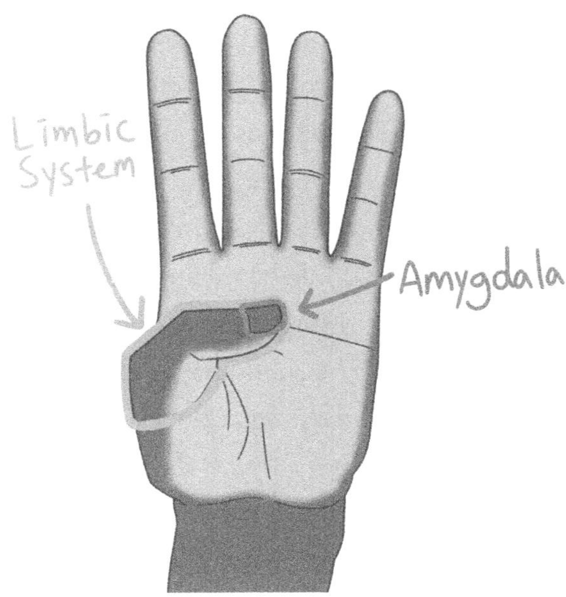

The amygdala processes information from the outside world: sights, sounds, smells, and so on. It does this in a split second and without your being conscious that it is doing it. The amygdala decides whether you are safe or not; it is especially oriented to noticing anything in your environment that's novel or unexpected and that could pose a threat to you. You might suddenly experience fear. Your heart might pound, or you may feel the urge to run or fight. That's your amygdala working to keep you safe by sending fear signals to your mind-body system.

The amygdala can be a big help. Let's say you are on a city sidewalk. Suddenly, a taxicab jumps the curb and is speeding in your direction. The rapid signal from your smoke detector, the amygdala, sends you into a flight response, and you leap out of the way. All of this happens without your consciously deciding to do it—it is automatic.

Imagine if you had stopped to think (that's your cortex) about what to do—what could have happened? If your cortex hadn't been offline due to surging stress chemicals from the fear of what is happening, it would have helped you respond with problem-solving: *I could jump to the left, or maybe the right would be better. Maybe I should drop to the ground and hope the taxi will pass over me.* But, in a fast-moving event like the taxi jumping the curb, what would happen to you while doing all that slow-process thinking? Yes, you'd be run over by the taxi.

TRIO OF DEFENSIVE RESPONSES: FIGHT, FLIGHT, FREEZE

All humans, as well as other animals, have brains that are wired with three automatic, or fast-brain, protection responses. Coming from the brain stem, they are called defensive responses. Like other functions from the brainstem that happen automatically, such as breathing and blinking, your defensive responses happen without any conscious thinking or decision-making on your part.

Defensive responses include the fight, flight, and freeze responses, which are generated without you deciding to use one of them. These three automatic responses each use fast-brain processing. If you go through a thought process that weighs your options, that's not a defensive response—it's slow-process decision-making.

Fast-brain processing occurs when your cortex (thinking brain) goes offline during highly charged situations, and you react instantly without taking time to think about various decisions or options. Fast-brain processing is your amygdala's way of saving your life by stopping the slow-brain processing that involves thinking through possible strategies.

FAST-BRAIN PROCESSING CAN HELP OR HURT

Sometimes fast-brain processing is good, and other times it's bad. It can save your life, but it might also create many problems for you. It all depends on the situation and how it happens. Let's take a deeper look.

Understanding the defensive responses and the fast-brain processing they rely on may help you also understand why you or others sometimes take an action that leads to trouble. You might not have *planned* to fight or flee—it happened automatically. Or someone automatically freezes when faced with a person who needs help. Sometimes this fast-brain processing is lifesaving, as in the taxicab story above, but the outcome isn't always positive.

If it happens with a police officer, for example, terrible things can happen. The police won't care if you say you couldn't get out of the car when ordered to (freeze response), didn't intend to run away (flight response), or didn't mean to raise your fists as an officer approached (fight response). "It just happened," unfortunately, is not likely to hold up in a court of law. I teach neuroscience to police departments, and I believe it is essential for those who police our communities to realize how brains—their own and others'—can respond when people are frightened.

Recently, several officers explained to me how they believe they know if someone is guilty of an offense. One said he knows a person is guilty when the person doesn't make eye contact with him. But making that assumption of guilt based on lack of eye contact is often incorrect. Failing to make eye contact when you are afraid can be a flight response and usually has nothing to do with deciding to do it. You aren't consciously in control of your eyes looking away when it is a defensive flight response—it happens automatically.

I told the officers about fast-brain processing and being sent into fight, flight, or freeze mode without consciously deciding it. I asked the officers for examples from their own experiences, and each had, of course, acted without thinking in many instances. Sometimes it can save your life, like ducking when you hear a loud sound. And sometimes it can have tragic results, like mindlessly starting to run when you are ordered to stop.

EXAMPLES FROM YOUR EXPERIENCE

Stop for a minute to reflect on this information. Can you think of a time when you were in any of these three defensive responses: fight, flight, or freeze? If you answered "yes," what triggered that defensive response in you? What happened as a result? Remember, it is *not* a defensive response if you made a conscious decision to do it. The three defensive responses all happen automatically, in a split second.

Let's take a deeper look at each of these three defensive responses that are wired into your brain stem.

The Fight Response

You can probably remember a time when you were having a problem with someone and consciously decided to let the person know how you felt. The key word in this last sentence is "decided." If you decide to get into a verbal or physical altercation with someone, you have used the thinking part of your brain, the cortex. You went through a thought process and made a decision. It may not necessarily have been a good decision, but you used your thinking capacity.

When you go into the defensive fight response, you act without thinking. It can mean raising your voice, or it can be physical aggression such as kicking or hitting. When in the defensive fight response, your amygdala has sensed you are at such a high risk of danger that you don't have time to think about options. Stress chemicals are rapidly released that block conscious decision-making. You launch into fight. Can you think of examples of the fight response you have experienced yourself or observed in others?

The Flight Response

Let's look at another example of a defensive response that is wired into your brain stem and happens automatically. The taxicab example is a good one, but the flight response can also show up as shutting your eyes to block out a scary sight or running away—or even cringing—when you hear a loud noise.

Have you ever gotten so mad at someone on a phone call that, without thinking, you just slammed the phone down? That's the flight response. Like the fight response, the flight response often occurs in personal relationships.

Imagine you are in a heated disagreement with someone very important to you, and the situation is escalating. The flight response could cause you (or the other person) to storm out of the room in a fury, hang up in the middle of a phone call, or even threaten to leave the relationship. The flight response gets you away from the situation as fast as possible. It is not a choice you make mindfully—it happens below your level of consciousness. People often regret these fast system defenses later when they come back into balance. Damage to the relationship may have occurred and may need to be cleaned up.

Some scientists believe excessive use of mind-altering substances is another example of the flight response. It blots out reality, so the user isn't suffering as much. Do you agree that this could be an example of a flight response? Not everyone does.

The Freeze Response

The freeze response is the most dangerous of the three defensive responses in its impact on your body because the stress chemicals that build up during high reactivity do not get discharged as they do with fighting or fleeing.

Stress chemicals are like the gas in your vehicle's tank. They fuel your actions. When they fuel the defensive response of fight or flight, the action uses up a lot of the stress chemicals, which get discharged from the body through your actions.

Full-Body Shutdown

Unlike fight and flight, the freeze response is a full-body shutdown. When someone is in a freeze response, the person often appears to be expressionless with eyes that look vacant. Someone in freeze mode usually feels numb and is unable to verbalize what's going on. The person can often still move physically, but emotions are deadened, and the voice sounds flat if the person speaks.

The body enters a freeze response when the amygdala perceives that you can't fight or flee. It's a last-resort response. Remember, like other defensive responses, this is not a response you choose. It happens automatically when your amygdala deems that you can't fight or flee.

Freeze is a very common response in children—if something bad or scary happens that they can't control, they may freeze. They are often unable to fight or flee because they are young and small, so the freeze response kicks in. Children in abusive situations often freeze. Adults do, too.

MARCHESA'S STORY
OF THE FREEZE RESPONSE

This story comes from my work with people fleeing Central America because of the drug cartels. Marchesa was just thirteen when she was raped by gang members in El Salvador. She and her family had experienced numerous incidents of violence, and they finally decided to attempt to come to the United States.

Border patrol agents caught Marchesa and placed her in a detention center. Eventually, she went before an immigration judge. During the questioning about what had happened to cause her to try to cross the border, she said four men had raped her. In a later round of questioning, she said it was five men. Because she had changed her story, the judge said she must be lying. He threw her case out and sent her back to El Salvador, saying she was not a credible witness.

This is an unfortunate instance of how those in the court systems are unaware of neuroscience and the freeze response. If, during the rape, Marchesa went into a freeze response because her amygdala perceived that she couldn't fight or flee, her memory could be missing some details of the rape.

This is called "reconstructed memory," and it happens when the stress chemicals that created the freeze response alter a person's recollection of details related to a traumatic event. Memory becomes fragmented and sometimes distorted, so the memories of what happened are not stored in an orderly way. Traumatic memories are often in a jumble, and some aspects of the event may even be permanently gone from the memory system. Marchesa wasn't lying. Instead, the freeze response impacted her recollection of the details of what happened.

DEFENSIVE DEFAULTS

We each have all three defensive responses wired into the brain stem. However, when a defensive response has occurred over a period of time, particularly in childhood, a time when we have few ways to protect ourselves, the one we used can become a default response that carries into adulthood. This means that when bad or challenging situations happen later in life, you are likely to default to the defensive response that was generated in childhood.

Think about that in your own life. Do you have a default defensive response when things are extremely upsetting?

THE BRAIN CAN SHRINK
DUE TO FEAR

Research shows that a certain structure in children's brains can actually shrink after repeated fear and trauma. Stress chemicals can kill brain cells. One reason kids may not remember some traumas from earlier in life is because stress chemicals killed the brain cells that held the memories.

The part of the brain that can shrink due to traumatic events is called the hippocampus. In Dan Siegel's hand brain model, in which the amygdala is your thumbnail, the hippocampus is the rest of your thumb. Take a look at where it is by opening your hand and putting your thumb across the palm of your hand. Your fingernail represents your amygdala, and the rest of your thumb represents the hippocampus.

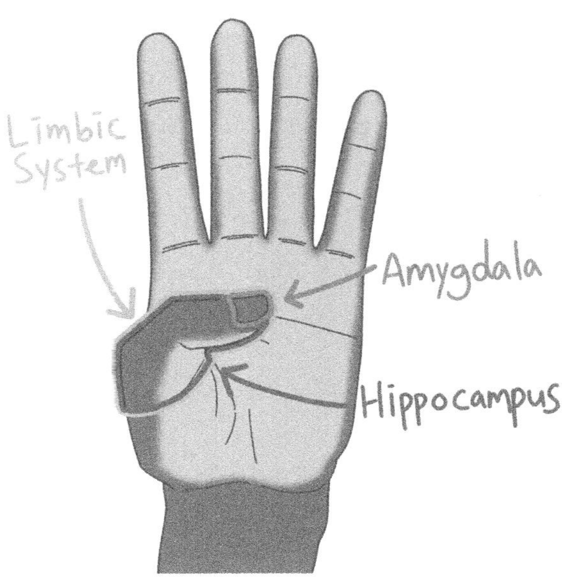

The hippocampus is an important brain structure to know about, in part because it is the place where your short-term memories are stored before being sent to other parts of the brain for long-term storage. Can you see why children and adults who have a history of traumatic events can have trouble learning and remembering? It's not due to a lack of intelligence. It can be due to the impact of trauma on brain cells, especially in the part of the brain that holds short-term memory. Fear generates stress chemicals, and stress chemicals can distort memory and kill brain cells.

The way your brain-body system receives information from the outside world is through sensory experience. The next chapter has important information about "sensory triggers." As you will see, some triggers are positive, and others are negative.

SENSORY TRIGGERS: SOMETIMES GOOD, SOMETIMES BAD

You've heard the word "trigger" before, but in neuroscience, the word has a very different meaning than the part of a gun. All of us experience triggers at times, some positive and others negative. Triggers are sensations—smells, sounds, tastes, sights, touch—that are linked inside your brain to experiences from the past. They can pop into your consciousness without you intentionally bringing them to mind. They can also be brought to mind purposefully. The BGP shows you how to manage triggers so they can work for you and not against you. It's an essential tool to have in your superpower tool kit.

Songs are common positive triggers for many people. Let's imagine you had a special song you loved to listen to when you were a teen. Maybe you knew all the words and sang along when you heard the song. As an adult, if you are listening to a podcast that includes that song, your body instantly responds with pleasure and maybe flashes of memories of dancing to that song or listening to it with friends. You didn't try to bring those memories to mind—they just popped into your consciousness.

That's what a trigger is: a sensory experience that can include images, feelings, and bodily responses connected to a positive or negative experience from the past.

This information about triggers can be reassuring to those who have been triggered in a negative way and perhaps done something embarrassing, like freeze or flee when that trigger appears. Since the negative reaction isn't connected to anything that is happening in the present moment, it can be distressing. Sometimes people don't even know the original negative experience that is causing their present reactions.

Remember, information is power, so knowing about triggers can help you understand that you are not crazy or wrong when you are negatively triggered. You'll learn to use the BGP skills to take away a negative trigger's power over you. You'll also learn how to use positive triggers to improve your life.

Let's look a bit more deeply at triggers.

POSITIVE TRIGGERS

Most of us have a bunch of positive triggers based on early life experiences. I'll share one that Janice described to me. Janice's grandmother raised her, and money was very limited in their household. But every now and then, Janice's grandmother bought the ingredients for her favorite sugar cookies. They were big and soft, not the crunchy kind. She would open the door after school, and her nose was hit with the wonderful smells of those cookies from the oven. Her grandma always let her have one as soon as the cookies were cool enough.

As an adult many years later, Janice was walking past a bakery that had its door open. Suddenly, that same special smell hit Janice's nostrils, transporting her back to her grandma's kitchen. It was as if she were really back with her—the sweet smells, the warmth of the kitchen, her grandma's flowered apron, a sense of calm and well-being. All of these sensory memories flooded back just from the smell of cookies baking that day at the bakery. She had such a sense of comfort and love! This is an example of a smell being a positive trigger.

And that smell then triggered images from the kitchen and warm, fuzzy feelings, too.

Think about the positive triggers from your early life. Many of us have a popular song we loved when we were younger. Whenever the song plays, we are transported back to that time in our lives. All kinds of smells from the past can be positive triggers. In the BGP, we refer to these positive triggers as "resources." I originally learned about resources from Peter Levine. You can intentionally bring up a memory that triggers calming sensations and positive emotions. And when you stay a while in those sensations by noticing more and more details of the experience and then shift your attention to where the sensations are strongest in your body, you'll be building a climate of health.

NEGATIVE TRIGGERS

Positive triggers offer a sense of well-being, but triggers are often negatively charged. Negative triggers can also come from various smells, sounds, or sights—but rooted in an unpleasant, frightening, or traumatic experience from your past.

Tracey was eighteen and a dutiful daughter. She took care of her younger siblings after school and helped her highly stressed mother in many other ways as well. One rainy night she was walking to the laundromat with two bags of laundry.

It was dark, and the street was mostly empty. About a block from the laundromat, a man grabbed Tracey from behind. She was raped and left crying at the curb. All she could remember about the rapist was that he wore a blue shirt.

From that point on, anytime Tracey was outside on a rainy night, her stomach tightened and her heart pounded. Darkness combined with the dampness of the rain had become a negative trigger for her. When those two things were present at the same time, her amygdala signaled danger. Even when she was in the company of other people, the same fear-based sensations flooded her body. She had to control herself not to run away.

Several years later, Tracey was in the grocery store, heading to the checkout line. Out of the corner of her eye, she saw a man in a blue shirt. Before she knew it, she abandoned her cart and ran out of the store. Most likely, the man in the grocery store wasn't the man who had raped her. But in that moment, the blue shirt was a traumatic trigger for her amygdala, and she went into a flight response.

People who experience traumatic triggers often say they feel crazy. They flee in fear when a situation isn't a real threat or go into a freeze response and shut down for no apparent reason. Many people don't even know they have traumatic triggers until something sets one off in the brain's memory system.

PART OF YOUR BRAIN'S MEMORY SYSTEM

Triggers come from all kinds of sensory experiences—visual images, smells, touch, sounds, and so on—that are stored in the brain's memory system below the level of consciousness. A person might only know they avoid certain situations (dark, rainy nights) because they experience unpleasant bodily distress (pounding heart, stomachache, shallow breathing).

The information from neuroscience, when coupled with the BGP practical skills, is a powerful tool kit for you to use in becoming the person you want to be. I hope you use the tool kit regularly. When you do, you'll be enlisting the amazing superpower neuroplasticity to build a better brain that works for you, not against you.

Chapter 5

NEUROPLASTICITY IS ONE OF YOUR SUPERPOWERS

It's hard to believe that as complex as your brain already is, you have a superpower that makes it possible to change your brain. The name of that superpower is "neuroplasticity," which is your brain's ability to be rewired by growing or deleting neurons. The brain can change for the better or for the worse.

Think of your brain as a cell phone that comes with a bunch of apps and the ability to add others. There are apps on your phone for an amazing number of purposes. Some apps are "factory default"—they're wired into every phone and can't be changed. Others have to be downloaded. The human brain is like that, too.

The defensive responses of fight, flight, and freeze are examples of default "apps" we are already wired with and will always have. But, as a result of traumatic events in a person's life, the defensive responses can get miscalibrated. Let's look at the fight response that is wired into your brain. If it has gotten miscalibrated by traumatic or negative events, you may launch into a fight response over situations that don't require such a heavy-duty response. Fortunately, because of neuroplasticity, we can correct the miscalibration. The BGP skills help you make changes for the better, and practice makes the changes stick.

Some of us have added so-called apps to the brain's wiring, such as drawing, being a math whiz, or knowing how to roller-skate. Some athletes have added special wiring for skills like shooting baskets, for example. The process that creates wiring something into your brain is, first, the act of paying attention to something you want to wire in and, second, practicing what you want to strengthen. That's what athletes do, and so can you.

Neuroplasticity and attention go hand in hand. What we pay attention to gets wired in. What we stop paying attention to gets pruned away. All of the BGP skills rely on managing where your attention goes.

PRACTICE MAKES PERFECT

Amazing US basketball player Steph Curry wasn't born with a basketball-shooting app. He grew that app by wiring it in with practice. He taught himself to shoot a three-pointer from outside the three-point line—he called it the "zone buster."

As a kid, he used to lie in bed and throw a balled-up sock as close to the ceiling as possible without letting the sock touch the ceiling—thousands of times. He probably did not know he was using neuroplasticity. He just got better and better at doing what he wanted to do.

Through neuroplasticity, you can change your own brain by controlling what you pay attention to and what you practice—and you can do it consciously, on purpose. Think of something you became skilled at by practicing. It might be a sport, dance steps, spelling, or even remembering important numbers. You don't exactly ace any of these the very first time. Only after repeated attempts does your brain begin to lay down the pathways (wiring) that make certain skills, behaviors, and learning styles seem to come with natural ease.

If Steph Curry were to quit basketball and not play again for a long time, his "zone buster" wiring would eventually be pruned away. Look at the graphic below. It shows an active neuron and an inactive neuron. One is bushy from attention and practice. The other shows what pruning looks like. We can all learn to prune away negative habits and responses and wire in good ones. That's great news!

Neuroplasticity is an exciting process. It means you have the power to create the brain you want. I want to help you harness that power!

HABITS ALSO WIRE THE BRAIN

We also create pathways in the brain through habits. We consciously maintain some habits, and others we maintain just because we're stuck in a rut. Do you have a not-so-good-for-you habit that you repeat because you don't pay enough attention to changing it? It's important to note that practice isn't always about wiring in the good stuff. It can also wire away the not-so-good stuff.

My friend Henry was a pessimist. I've always liked Henry, but he regularly showed his pessimism. He applied for a job and said, "I know they'll give it to someone else." Another time we attended a talk at a university. Henry focused only on what he didn't like about the environment: "The chairs are uncomfortable," "The room is too hot," "I can't even see the speaker." His negativity cast a shadow over his good qualities. I sometimes made excuses to avoid hanging out with him.

Pessimism was a habit that was wired into Henry's brain through repetition. Bad habits are an example of neuroplasticity working in a way that has negative outcomes. To prune pessimism away, Henry would have to stop paying attention to what's negative for him in every situation. Henry was losing friends because many of them, myself included, were tired of his pessimistic attitude.

We came up with a plan. We decided that whenever Henry acted pessimistic or negative, we would walk away from him, look the other way, and not respond. And, whenever Henry was not stuck in pessimism, we would act engaged and interested. Because the brain craves positive social relationships, Henry's pessimism decreased in less than a month because of our negative reinforcement. We helped Henry begin to wire away the pessimism. Once Henry was in on our strategy, he got on board himself. He began catching himself just as he was about to say something negative.

RETRAINING YOUR BRAIN

We let Henry in on our little experiment. At first, he was annoyed, but then he saw the affection behind it. Henry mattered to all of us. But his pessimism had become an unconscious habit that made him unpleasant to be around.

Once the habit was weakened, Henry consciously took control of stopping himself when he started to say something pessimistic. He stopped the comment and replaced it with something neutral or even positive. I'm happy to say he is no longer a pessimist. He pruned that habit away by regularly shifting his attention to something neutral or positive. He retrained his brain! That's neuroplasticity in action. It's a superpower we all have.

Through practice and focused attention, you, too, can enlist your brain's ability to change. Try this neuroplasticity exercise:

1. Bring to mind a negative reaction or behavior you have that you or someone in your life doesn't like.
   a. My negative reaction is ________________
   ____
   _____________________________________.

2. What would be a more skillful response to replace that negative one?
   a. A more skillful response would be ________
   ____
   _____________________________________.

3. Choose an "interrupter word" that you can say to signal to yourself that a bad habit is about to happen. That way, you can interrupt it before it happens.
   a. My interrupter word is ________________.

4. Each time the negative reaction is about to happen, say your interrupter word in your mind or softly out loud, and then shift to your more skillful response.

When you practice this process for several weeks, you enlist your brain's neuroplasticity, and before too long, you will have wired in the new, improved response and pruned away the old one. If you find the negative behavior creeps back after a while, which it is likely to do, just resume your use of the interrupter word. Practice will wire it in again.

A sports physiologist said it this way: "Where your attention goes, energy flows, and that's what grows." The BGP is about taking charge of where your attention goes. Rewiring your brain is as simple as that. Attention is an important superpower you can have in your tool kit.

More about the power of attention is in the next chapter.

Chapter 6

ATTENTION IS ANOTHER SUPERPOWER

Has this ever happened to you? You were minding your own business and, all of a sudden, a stern voice shouted, "Pay attention!" Maybe it was a parent, a teacher, or even a partner.

Most of us have heard those words at least a few times since we were kids. Usually, it's said in a harsh, critical, or disdainful tone of voice. *Pay attention to the teacher, pay attention to the weather so you can dress properly, pay attention to oncoming traffic, pay attention to learning your multiplication tables, pay attention to your finances, and on and on and on.*

THE SUPREME COMMANDER
OF WHO YOU ARE

Over the many years of trying to pay attention to all you were told to pay attention to, it's almost certain no one shared with you the most important way to pay attention. There is a way that is the most powerful mechanism for you to become exactly who you want to be—emotionally, thoughtfully, creatively, career-wise, and health-wise.

Sounds sort of crazy, right? Maybe you think I'm exaggerating, but I'm not. This way of paying attention will help you create an exciting, generative personal and professional life. And, as if that weren't enough, in the process, you'll be rewiring your brain by practicing. That's using the amazing gift of neuroplasticity, which makes life-altering brain changes that can decrease reactivity and enhance the qualities you want to "stick" with you.

PAYING ATTENTION
PAYS OFF

The kind of attention I'm talking about—drumroll now because, trust me, it is that special—is called *Sensory Attention*. Sensations are bodily responses like heat, trembling, tightness, coldness, pain, and many others we often ignore. At the end of this book is a list of sensation words that describe positive and negative sensations, including traumatic sensations. The list can be helpful as you learn to pay attention at the sensory level. By the way, if you're like me and want *proof* of a new concept you haven't heard about before, let me remind you that this information about the power of attention to change your brain comes from neuroscience research.

Remember Siegel's hand brain model? Each of the three parts of your brain has a different way of processing the world. The cortex processes information via thinking, so its "language" is thoughts. The limbic system, or middle brain, processes through feelings, so its language is emotions. But the brain stem is the focus in the BGP because its language is sensations—the most fundamental way we have of processing experiences.

Learning how to pay attention or track the sensations in your body gives you the power to decide whether to keep your attention where it is or shift it to something else that will create a positive change. We explore more of the power of shifting attention in Chapter 8, which features the BGP skills.

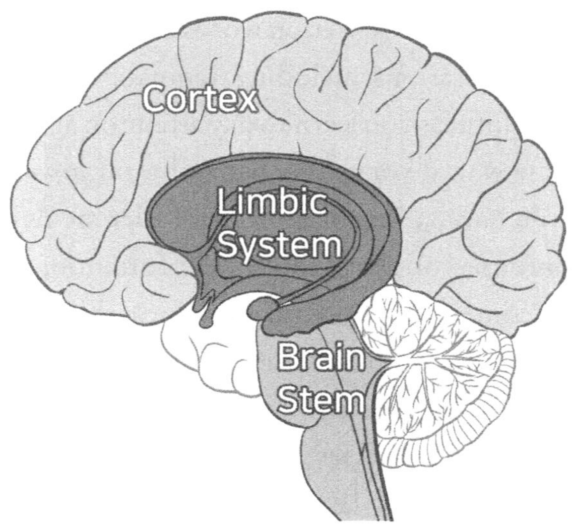

Everything comes into your brain-body system first as a sensation, and then it gets sent along to the middle (limbic) and upper (cortex) brain, where it is rapidly—so fast you don't even notice it happening—translated into thoughts and feelings. That's why the BGP focuses on sensation—the most basic and fundamental part of the human experience.

PAYING ATTENTION AT THE SENSORY LEVEL

When you learn to control the sensory level of your experience by paying attention to sensations in your body, you also take control of your emotions and thoughts, since they originate from sensations at the brain stem level.

I'm sure you've had the sensation of your stomach growling. That sensory experience gets translated into a decision in your cortex. You decide whether to ignore the sensation or find something to eat, as well as what it will be and when and where you'll get it. That sensory signal from your stomach generates a series of thoughts. Feelings may also be generated, such as the feelings that you can't get what you want to eat, or you are trying to lose weight and feel guilty that you want ice cream, etc.

Most of us are pretty good at naming at least some of our emotions, and we can usually describe what we are thinking. But few have learned to pay attention to what I call the "language of sensation." And yet, it's like a secret power. Sensory attention is essential, and you'll become an expert at not only paying attention at the sensory level but also at using practical skills to manage and change sensations for the better. When the sensations change, so do your thoughts and feelings.

Negative sensations can fill your body with toxic stress chemicals that cause you to become reactive and even physically sick. But you can shift your attention in a way that builds calming, positive sensations that help you think clearly and make good decisions. At the heart of the matter—in creating a brain that supports the life you want and a climate of health in your body—is *noticing* what's happening inside at the sensory level and then deciding what to do with what you notice.

Thanks to ever-improving neuroimaging techniques—taking pictures of the brain as it works on tasks—we know a lot about how the brain works. From the research that maps the brain at work, we know how the brain and other parts of the nervous system work together, controlling communication networks that shape our body processes such as blood pressure, breathing, heart rate, and much more.

This kind of research shows what happens inside your brain-body system at the *level of sensation*—body temperature, trembling, tightness, pain, and numbness, for example. Look over that chart of the different kinds of sensations at the end of the book. Some words describe positive and pleasureful sensations, and others describe negative sensations that turn into emotions like fear, anger, sadness, and more.

BGP skills will help you develop a sensory awareness so you can make good decisions about what to do with what you're noticing. Otherwise, you'll be on the autopilot that has developed over the years of your life. Some of that autopilot may be fine—or at least neutral—but some may be what is keeping you from being the person you want to be.

As you learn how to use the BGP's attention-based skills, you'll become an expert—not only at paying attention at the sensory level, but also at using the practical skills to increase and strengthen positive sensations that create a climate of health in your body, including clarity of thinking. You'll learn to shift attention away from sensations that fill your body with toxic stress chemicals and put it on what will build sensations of calm.

Chapter 7

WHAT—AND WHERE—IS MY RZONE?

In this chapter, you'll learn about a zone of the brain and other nervous system functioning that I call the "resilient zone," or RZone. You can be your best self when you are inside your RZone. Inside the RZone you have clear thinking, you don't act impulsively, and your body is not getting flooded with stress chemicals.

Everyone has an RZone, but most people don't know about it, much less pay attention to it or even realize that we can control how deep it is. The RZone is always operating and determining how we make decisions and respond to whatever life deals us.

Ready for an information power surge? Let's get started with a few basics about your RZone.

KEEPING REACTIVITY
IN CHECK

Staying inside your RZone is essential to your physical and emotional health and well-being. When you are inside that RZone, you can be your best self. But it's more than just a "happy place." Your RZone is the zone of functioning where you can think strategically, consider consequences, make a sensible plan, remember facts, acknowledge mistakes, and be a good friend.

You can be sad or mad when you're inside your RZone but not to the degree that you lose your ability to think clearly and strategically. And inside the RZone, you aren't sad or mad at such a high level that you fill your body with toxic stress chemicals.

When that high level of reactivity happens, I call it "getting bumped out of your RZone." When this happens, toxic stress chemicals take a toll on you after about twenty minutes, and the defensive responses of fight, flight, and freeze can kick in. You are in reactive mode, not thinking clearly or strategically, and you may take actions or behave in ways you later regret.

A DEEP OR SHALLOW RZONE

While everyone has one, RZones are not all the same size. Some people have a deep RZone, and it takes a major stressor—or a lot of stressors at the same time—to bump them out of their zone. Others have a shallow RZone, where even a minor stressor (such as spilling coffee) flips them out of the zone.

Do you think you generally have a deep, shallow, or average RZone? It isn't a fixed band of functioning. It can vary based on your experiences due to neuroplasticity. For example, some people have a deep RZone related to some experiences but a shallow one related to others. An example from my life is that I have a shallow RZone when I am going through transitions. I get cranky and less organized. I've learned over the years to anticipate my reactivity to transitions, and I use the BGP skills to keep myself in the RZone. I practice what I preach!

YOU'VE GOT RHYTHM!

The natural world is full of many rhythms and cycles: the day following the night, the seasons changing throughout the year, the moon's phases, the tides. We have cycles and rhythms inside our bodies as well. The RZone is about a rhythm between two important branches of your nervous system—the sympathetic and parasympathetic branches. These two oddly named branches impact every organ in your body, so they are very important to your health and well-being.

The Sympathetic Branch

Think of a car for a minute. When you push on the car's accelerator, that's like the sympathetic branch of your nervous system. It activates you. Your heart rate increases, your breathing gets shallower, and stress chemicals begin to flow. Your body is preparing for action. This sympathetic activation is a good thing as long as it stays at a level that's inside your RZone. You can tell it's at a level that's inside the zone because your heart won't be pounding strongly, you will still be able to think about what to do about what has just happened, and your muscles won't be tensed up. When the activation stays inside the RZone, it's your vitality. It provides fuel for getting things done.

But when the sympathetic activation is so strong or extreme that it bounces you out of your RZone, negative things can happen. The amount of stress chemicals produced can block your ability to think clearly, so you might make impulsive decisions. And being bumped out of your RZone for more than twenty to thirty minutes hurts your immune system and, over time, can cause serious physical and emotional health problems.

Stress chemicals give your immune system a positive boost as long as they don't stay in your body for longer than twenty to thirty minutes. Here's a positive example of sympathetic activation. Imagine you are on a city street, and down the block, you spot a person you like a lot and hadn't expected to see. Your sympathetic branch activates with excitement. The closer you get, the more excited you become. And you can tell that your friend is also excited by looking at the expression on his or her face. Positive activation is good for you. It's your vitality, your life force, the fuel in the car.

The important point is that even negative activation doesn't usually result in long-term problems or high reactivity as long as it's at a level that lets you stay in your RZone.

The Parasympathetic Branch

The parasympathetic branch of the nervous system is like activating the car's brakes. It slows you down, calming you. As you and your familiar friend move closer to each other on that city block, the parasympathetic branch comes into play. It creates pleasurable sensations, deeper breathing, relaxed muscles, and a sense of well-being and positive anticipation.

The two branches work in a rhythm with each other throughout the day and night. Take a look at the graphic below. When the curve is rising, that's activation from the sympathetic branch. When the curve is going down, it's calming from the parasympathetic branch.

RESILIENT ZONE

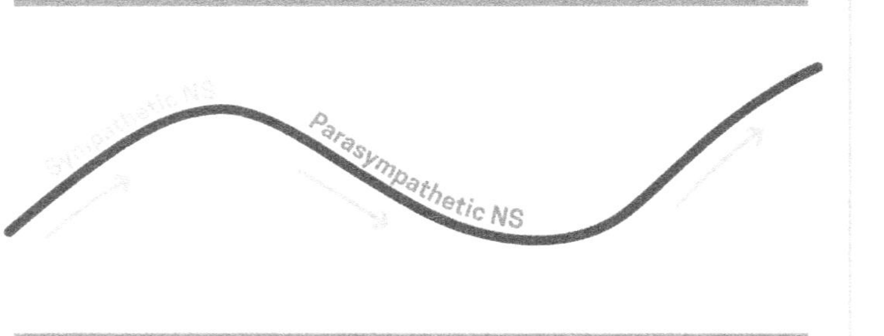

Inside the RZone you can be your best self

© 2012 Threshold GlobalWorks

This rhythm between the two branches goes on all the time, all day and night, but we seldom pay attention to it. It's similar to eye blinking—you don't notice it unless you specifically decide to notice it. That's how the RZone rhythm is, too. It usually operates below our level of consciousness.

We can control eye blinking if we want to, and we can also influence the rhythm of the sympathetic and parasympathetic branches if we pay attention to what's happening inside the body at the sensory level. Is your heart beating faster? Is muscle tension increasing? Those are signs of sympathetic activation. Managing your attention is one of your superpowers. Learn to manage where your attention goes, and you'll be able to tell if you're starting to move out of your RZone and then use BGP skills to get back in before reactivity takes over. You can be in charge of the kind of person you want to be. It just requires you to pay attention.

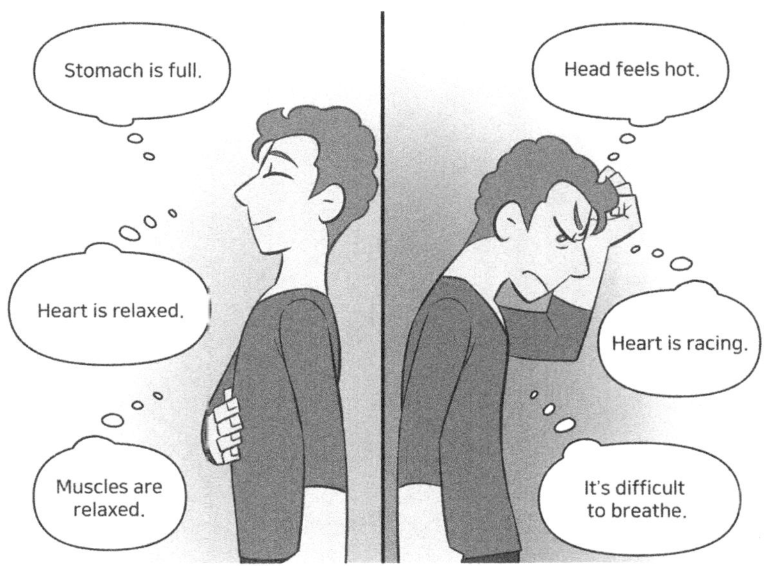

WHEN SOMETHING THREATENING HAPPENS

When something unexpected and threatening happens to you, your amygdala sends a big fear-based warning to your nervous system. The sympathetic branch spikes either far above or far below the RZone. The graphic below illustrates this, giving some examples of what can happen when you are bumped out above the RZone (called "being stuck on high") and when you are bumped out below the RZone ("being stuck on low").

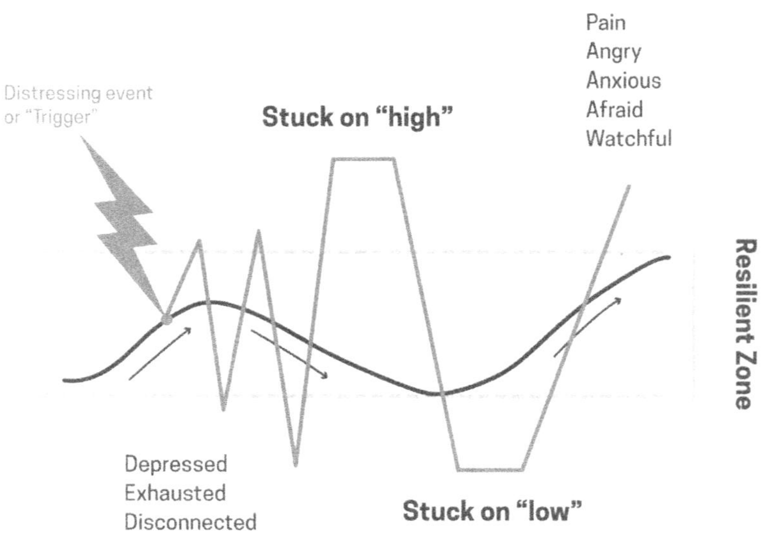

Some people get stuck only on high when they get bumped out of the RZone, and others get stuck only on low. Other people bounce between high and low, which can lead to the misdiagnosis of bipolar disorder, a mental illness characterized by extreme mood swings.

Bipolar disorder is a legitimate diagnosis when a biochemical imbalance is present, and medication can help treat it. But when bumping high and low is due to distressing or traumatic events, it is not likely to be bipolar disorder, and the BGP skills can help manage the reactivity.

THE IMPACT OF TRAUMA ON CHILDREN

Children also experience getting bumped out of the RZone, especially when frightening things occur. A child who bounces between high and low might be improperly diagnosed with attention deficit hyperactivity disorder (ADHD). As with adults, if the bumping high and low is due to a biochemical imbalance, ADHD can be a legitimate medical diagnosis, and the child may benefit from medication. But when the bumping high and low is due to past and present traumatic events, ADHD could be a misdiagnosis.

When children with trauma histories are misdiagnosed, they often do not receive the help and support they need.

Trauma can result in reactivity and a range of acting-out behaviors (stuck on high) or shutting down and exhibiting withdrawal behaviors (stuck on low). When teachers do not understand how trauma shows up in children, they may punish or criticize the child for behaviors instead of helping the child feel safe and protected.

Here's an example. I was presenting at a conference called "Children and the Law." I was describing the problem of ADHD misdiagnosis in children with trauma histories. During the break, a teacher came up to me and told me about a fourteen-year-old student who was in foster care. She expressed concerns that he may have intellectual disabilities and noted, "He just can't seem to learn."

I asked her what she knew about this boy's background. She described a series of awful events in his life that started when he was a toddler and was locked in a dark closet for three days. This was followed by other instances of abuse and neglect. Trauma has a big impact on the developing brains of children. The hippocampus can actually shrink, and that affects memory and learning. Doesn't it make sense that this boy's learning problems as a teen might be related to his trauma history? Of course it does.

This adolescent needs help, but this does not necessarily mean he is intellectually disabled. He needs consistent experiences of feeling safe and loved. Fortunately, the brain is a very resilient organ. It can change for the better with proper attention. Neuroplasticity is a human superpower!

Now, you have all of the neuroscience building blocks that are the foundation of the BGP. This foundation is an essential part of your tool kit for managing life's heavy lifting. It will help you understand the purpose of each BGP skill in the next chapter and why we use them the way we do. Once you have the neuroscience concepts and the BGP skills, you'll have a full tool kit to build your resilience and decrease reactivity and stress chemicals!

Chapter 8

BRAIN GAIN PROGRAM (BGP) SKILLS ARE AN ESSENTIAL PART OF YOUR TOOL KIT

Now for the skills! Peter Levine, a scientist and trauma expert, originally developed a version of these skills for clinicians to use with individuals who have experienced trauma. I've adapted Levine's skills for nonclinical use and changed one (Shift and Stay) so ordinary people, even kids, can use them nonclinically in a self-guided manner. Each skill relies on sensory attention. They are excellent as a wellness practice for interrupting reactivity and, through practice, rewiring your brain for a deeper RZone.

For many years now, I have been teaching my neuroscience-based model throughout the world. It can be used worldwide because every human has the same brain structures and processes. Until recently, I called it the Social Resilience Model (SRM). But as I began to write this book, I decided the model deserved a name that better reflects what it does, and the BGP was born. "Brain gain" is a good way to describe how people can harness and manage their sensory attention—use neuroscience concepts and skills—to gain a better-functioning brain!

SELF-CREATE TO BE GREAT!

I've taught this practical program to mental health practitioners, as well as to a wide array of individuals, groups, and organizations that simply wanted to break free from patterns of behavior and attitudes that blocked their highest potential. This program provides a way to self-create as a highly functioning person who succeeds at work and home.

The program has been put to the toughest of tests—used by first responders, including police officers and firefighters, as well as active military personnel and veterans. I've also taken the BGP to countries suffering after large-scale trauma such as hurricanes (United States), earthquakes (China, Nepal, Haiti), tsunamis (Thailand), and even genocide and other human-caused disasters (Rwanda, Kenya). It has been used with hundreds of people, some of whom have suffered trauma and others who haven't, who want to take charge, in this practical way, of living a better life.

It has been possible to do my work across cultures because the BGP is not limited to a particular culture. It doesn't rely on insight. It is skills-based, so it can be taught across various cultures and diverse groups. Because every human, regardless of where in the world they live, has a brain and nervous system designed the same way. We all have the capacity to create greater resilience—even in the face of challenging and frightening situations.

Are you ready to plunge in and create a brain that works better for you? Are you ready to cut off the flood of stress chemicals that toxifies your body? Ready to transform your reactivity to past hurts and present challenges, have more nourishing relationships, and be a better strategic thinker when faced with stress? As you go through the skills, notice that each one relies on taking charge of your attention, which is key to your success.

BGP SKILL 1:
SENSORY TRACKING

The first skill, Sensory Tracking (Tracking for short), trains you to pay attention to how your body responds to whatever is happening. This enables you to decide if you want to keep your attention where it is or shift to something that's better for you.

Tracking focuses on your body's sensations because they come from the brain stem and are the most basic way to create changes that last. Nothing comes into your brain-body system as a thought or feeling. All information initially comes in as sensation. Then, the sensations are almost instantaneously translated by the brain into emotions and thoughts. When you notice a particular thought or feeling, the first step is to see which sensations are the basis of that thought. Ask yourself, *What do I notice inside my body when I have this thought?* You might notice a faster heartbeat and rising muscle tension. That's the start of a negative process. You can then use the skills to build calming sensations. In just a quick minute or two you have avoided a surge of stress chemicals and helped yourself stay or return to the RZone.

You can control your thoughts, emotions, and behaviors if you **pay attention** to what they are doing inside your body at the sensory level. Are you acting in a way that is calming? Are your thoughts revving you up in a good way or in a bad way? Do you feel like shutting down? Did you just say or do something that hurts you or someone else? If you don't pay attention to what's happening at the sensory level, your amygdala will run the show. And your amygdala has a negativity bias—always on the alert for potential threats.

By paying attention to what's happening inside your body at the sensory level, you become the commander of your well-being because sensory experience shapes thoughts and feelings.

Let's try Tracking and see what you notice. You don't need to *change* anything. This is just a chance to get to know your body at the sensory level:

1. Take a minute to just notice your breath going in and out. Focus your attention on the rise and fall of your chest. Notice that the breathing is happening without any effort on your part. Is the breath shallow? Deep? Quick? Tight?
2. Now shift your attention to your body. Is it relaxed? Is there tightness anywhere? Where do you feel the most relaxed? Just notice.
3. Finally, just put your attention to the top of your head and then let your attention slowly drift down

your body, noticing any sensations that arise—
all the way down to your feet.

Tracking is an essential skill for self-management. Tracking as you go through your day is a good way to practice. Every BGP skill uses Tracking. That's how you decide whether to strengthen a positive sensation or shift away from a negative one.

BGP SKILL 2: GROUNDING

The second skill, Grounding, is an ancient tool used in many healing traditions. Grounding is great for creating a climate of health in your body by generating parasympathetic (calming) sensations. The essence of Grounding is to put your attention on the support of a solid surface against your body—the floor under your feet, a wall against your back, a chair against your legs, the mattress supporting your body. This stability creates parasympathetic sensations, which are calming, and builds a sense of safety so the amygdala can settle down and not be so vigilant.

Try this exercise that uses the first two BGP skills—Tracking and Grounding—to manage your attention. The exercise is about taking control of where your attention is focused (Grounding) and then noticing what happens inside your body at the sensory level (Tracking). Read through the whole exercise before you start, and then go back to the beginning and follow each step.

1. Find a comfortable place to sit and settle in, letting your eyes casually drift around the room. Do not focus on anything in particular, but just remind yourself that you are right here, right now.

2. Next, put your attention to the support of the floor under your feet. Really sense that solidness underfoot.

3. As you put your attention on the floor that supports your feet, what do you notice inside your body at the sensory level? How about your breathing—does it get faster or slower, or does it stay about the same? Is there more or less muscle tension as you notice the floor supporting your feet, or is the tension about the same?

4. Now, shift your attention to any places on your body that are supported by the chair. How about your back? Sense the support of the chair against your back, and as in the last step, notice what happens inside your body as you put your attention on your back—your breathing, muscle tension, or other physical responses.

5. Last, let your attention drift around your body, noticing any places that feel more relaxed or are at least neutral. Let your attention stay with a place on your body that feels the calmest or most

relaxed. Hold your attention there for a minute or two.

Don't worry if it is hard to notice the sensations the first few times you try Grounding and Tracking. These are new skills for you, so it can take some practice before significant results kick in. As you practice them, you'll wire in your ability to notice sensations and your body's ability to respond to the skills.

You can use Grounding when you're ready for sleep by focusing your attention on the support of the mattress or pillow. Notice each and every place on your body that is supported—the back of your head, your shoulders, your back, your legs. Then use Tracking to notice the calming sensations that build. Pay attention to how your body experiences the calming, such as a deeper breath, muscles relaxing, or slowed heart rate. Some people describe the relaxation that comes from Grounding as a positive heaviness in the body. Others describe a feeling of lightness. These sensations show that tension is fading away.

Of course, you can use Grounding and Tracking in the daytime, too. There are many ways to ground yourself, and as is true with all five skills, no one needs to know you're using them. You can do all the skills with your eyes open. You can also do them with your eyes closed when you're by yourself.

Some people find it easier to keep their attention focused on sensations when they close their eyes.

One friend calls these the "stealth skills" because no one needs to know you're doing them. For example, if you are noticing, or Tracking, yourself getting agitated when you're in a conversation or situation, you can simply use Grounding to shift your attention away from your agitation and instead put your attention on the support of a solid surface. This can keep you from getting bumped out of your RZone. It also will help your thinking stay clear so you can decide what you want to do about the conversation or situation.

You can try it now. If you are reading this in a chair, on a seat on the bus—anywhere—just put your attention on a part of your body that is supported by a solid surface. Focus all your attention on the sensory experience of stability. And as you control your attention by focusing on that solid surface, pay attention to any sensations of calming that occur. Does your breath get a bit deeper? Do you notice any muscles relaxing? Anything else you notice?

Remember, noticing your body at a sensory level can take some practice. That's not typically how we go through the day, but as you do, periodically ask yourself, *What am I noticing inside my body at the sensory level?* You'll be training your attention. And practice—because of your brain's superpower, neuroplasticity—strengthens your ability to become skilled at Sensory Tracking.

Just a side note on Grounding: if you have trouble going to sleep or you wake in the night, the skill of Grounding can help you get back to sleep. After you use Grounding for a few nights, your sleep should improve because you're growing new pathways for calming in your brain. You'll be much better able to stay calm in activating situations, and that's a good thing!

BGP SKILL 3: RESOURCING

The third BGP skill is Resourcing. It partners with Skill 4, Resource Strengthening. Resources are the things in our lives that bring a sense of joy, gratitude, security, and pleasure—the positives that make life a blessing. A pleasing resource can be as simple as the smell of your morning coffee or as significant as the best thing that ever happened to you. Bring some of your resources to mind now, and write them in the spaces below. You'll be using these again.

My Resources

1. ____

2. ____

3. ____

4. ____

Like Grounding, the skill of Resourcing builds calming, parasympathetic sensations. These are the sensations that produce a climate of health in your body. Resourcing takes the amygdala's focus away from its negativity bias. This is important because negativity builds sympathetic activation, generates stress chemicals, and interferes with clear thinking.

Become a Resourcing Expert

Most of us have in our lives people, events, and activities, like those you've listed above, that bring a sense of joy, calmness, pleasure, and security. A favorite resource might be a place in nature, a person, a pet, or a delicious food. It can be something in the present or something from your past. It might even be in your imagination, such as a safe-place image or an imaginary friend. Follow these steps for an exercise in using the skill of Resourcing:

1. Bring a pleasurable resource to mind.
2. Put your full attention to all the various details that make this a pleasing resource for you. Are there positive smells, visual details, or pleasant sounds? If it is a person, where is your favorite place to be with that person? This is the skill of Resource Strengthening (further explained below), where you wallow around in all the many details of your resource, so the parasympathetic sensations have a chance to grow stronger and stronger.
3. As you bring up all the sensory details about this resource, notice your body's physical sensations— your heart rate, your breathing, and muscle tension.

Like with Grounding, it may take a bit of practice before you notice parasympathetic sensations of calming. It can take some time for your amygdala to realize you are taking charge of where your attention goes. So, stick with it. You'll be enlisting your neuroplasticity superpower that comes with practice. And before long, your amygdala will cooperate by allowing the parasympathetic sensations to build.

BGP SKILL 4:
RESOURCE STRENGTHENING

Resource Strengthening, the fourth BGP skill, partners with Resourcing, which is the skill you just learned. Since the amygdala strongly focuses on anything that could be a threat to you, to override that focus, you need to direct attention to more than one detail about your resource. One detail alone won't build enough of the parasympathetic sensations to build calmness and override negativity. You need to bring to mind a lot of details—at least three or four—about your resource. Bask in all the elements that make it a resource for you. This attention to multiple details of your resource is called Resource Strengthening.

There are scripts at the end of the book in the Bonus Chapter for Grounding, Resourcing, and Resource Strengthening. They will help you until you can follow the process on your own. The scripts can also be used by you to help other people learn the skills of Grounding, Resourcing, and Resource Strengthening.

How Marija Uses Resourcing in the Workplace

Marija's grandmother, Ana, who is from Slovenia, is an excellent cook. She now lives near Marija in New York City. Ana takes care of Marija's children while Marija works, and she has taught the children all the songs she sang when Marija was a child.

Marija uses the pair of skills—Resourcing and Resource Strengthening—when she is having a hard day at work. She sits quietly at her desk and brings Ana's face to mind. She then strengthens that resource by bringing to mind all the wonderful things about her grandmother—the smell of her perfume, all the objects Ana brought from Slovenia, the sound of Ana's voice singing special songs, and the image of her children sitting against Ana as they listen to a story.

This takes only a few minutes, and no one at work can even tell Marija is practicing Resourcing and Resource Strengthening. Marija notices a growing sense of relaxation spreading throughout her body. She feels more settled, and the agitation dissipates. She is able to return her attention back to her work, stay focused, and maintain a sense of competency.

By shifting her attention from the negative work frustration to a resource and then strengthening it, Marija takes charge of her amygdala and cuts off the stress chemicals. She creates balance in her nervous system. It is simple yet so powerful. When you take control of where you focus your attention, you become the commander of your mind and make an important contribution to a healthy mind and body.

SKILL 5:
SHIFT AND STAY

Like the other four BGP skills, the skill of Shift and Stay relies on your taking control of where you direct your attention. Since the amygdala has a negativity bias, it pulls your attention to any unexpected events around you or anything that elicits negative emotions (like fear) or thoughts such as, *I'll never be as good as she is.*

This kind of negativity can bump you out of your RZone or interfere with your thinking strategically about how to handle a challenge. Shift and Stay can also help when a negative connection to your past triggers you.

Imagine you have overslept and are now running late for an appointment. You rush around, trying to get dressed, grab something to eat, and get out the door. But you can't find your belt or your phone. You become increasingly distraught and frustrated. Using this neuroscience-based skill called Shift and Stay, you shift your attention away from what is distressful and direct your focus to something that calms you. An easy place to shift to is to something you are grateful for. Gratitude is a powerful emotion that builds parasympathetic sensations.

Practical Options for Shift and Stay

Shift and Stay is a very simple way to manage reactivity and decrease the production of stress chemicals. You need only to notice the rise of reactivity or activation in your body and then shift your attention in a way that restores balance. It's as easy as that. But as easy as it is, it requires you first to be alert to the reactivity, to where the amygdala is sending your attention, so you can take control and shift your focus to something that brings balance back to your nervous system.

- One way you can apply the skill of Shift and Stay is by Grounding. You shift your attention away from your sensations of distress and focus on the support of the floor under your feet or your body being supported as you sit in a chair. Focus on places in your body that begin to relax. Notice your breathing as it slows down. Feel muscle tension lessening across your shoulders. You are coming back into your RZone.

- You could also use Resourcing and Resource Strengthening. You shift your attention away from your distress over being late by bringing to mind your little boy—how sweet he is when he gets into his pajamas at night. You further envision his little smile with the missing teeth and how he snuggles with you. You bring to mind all the factors that make him a resource for you. Then, use Tracking to notice signs of parasympathetic calming in your body. All of this can be done in two to three minutes, especially if you have trained your attention by regularly applying these skills.

- A third way you could use Shift and Stay is to just let your attention go to something in the room that has a positive association for you. Maybe it's a photo of a happy experience. Bring your full attention to that memory—that's a resource—and then strengthen the resource by bringing to mind several details about the experience, including smells, sights, and people you love. Then apply Sensory Tracking to notice the calming sensations that arise.

Once you are in your RZone, you have a far better chance of finding your belt and phone. You can think clearly and make a plan for what to do in the event you're late to your appointment.

"Shift and Stay" Away from Physical Pain

The skill of Shift and Stay can be effectively used to help alleviate physical pain. My friend had surgery on her right knee for a torn meniscus. She was in a lot of pain postsurgery, which interfered with her sleep at night. In addition to recommending Grounding and Resourcing to build parasympathetic sensations, I suggested she use Shift and Stay.

She practiced shifting her attention away from the pain in her knee to her other knee, which had no pain. She kept her attention there for a few minutes and then let her attention shift to any other places in her body that didn't have pain. She was amazed that she could fall asleep more easily after using this skill.

CONTROLLING WHERE YOUR ATTENTION GOES

The five skills you have just learned all focus on helping you decide where to direct your attention. You shift attention away from what is creating reactivity—where your amygdala wants you to be—to things that bring calm. This shift of attention interrupts the production of stress chemicals, helps you think more clearly, and decreases negative emotional responses. When you do this, you are creating a climate of health in your body.

And, when practiced, because of the wonders of neuroplasticity, you can change your brain. You'll change your brain from one that is reactive to every negative instance over the course of a day to a brain that can stay steady and effectively problem-solve.

Chapter 9

LIFE'S POTHOLES AND A PLAN TO MANAGE THEM

The street outside my office has several big potholes. From the window I can see cars giving a big jolt as they hit them. One day a man's tire went into the pothole with such an impact that the tire blew out and he had to be towed off the road.

All of us encounter potholes in our lives … some are small and are annoying but do no damage. Others are so large they make a negative impact in our lives … maybe by destroying a relationship. Maybe by causing so much stress that our health is affected.

Now that you know the key neuroscience concepts that are the building blocks for using the BGP's skills, let's look at how to step around life's potholes by using the practical skills. What do you know about your life's potholes? A pothole is one of those problems in your life that happens repeatedly. It often feels like you have no control over the potholes, but you do.

DANYA'S POTHOLE

Danya is a woman who has a lot of career skills and drive. She was determined to get a job as a senior staffer at an agency. She prepared herself by gaining relevant work-related experiences and followed a course of action that would make her competitive in the field. And she got the job.

But within a few months, the people working on Danya's team were making negative comments to her boss. They said Danya had an anger problem, and one staff member even said she was punitive and shaming. The boss asked for a meeting with Danya, who became belligerent and defensive. Danya was terminated from the job she had worked so hard to get.

DANYA'S MISSING STEP

Danya skipped over an important step in her job preparation. She had a reactivity problem she had never owned up to—it was always someone else's fault. She left a job a few years before because she had created a similar dynamic with people working under her supervision.

Danya's reactivity pothole was a deep one. She had fallen into the reactivity pothole before—actually, on more than several occasions. She was reactive not only at work but also with certain family and church members. She always attributed it to someone else's behavior.

How do you relate to Danya's story? Do you have a repetitive pothole in your life—some dynamic you react to that almost always ends badly? Using the Brain Gain skills, you can avoid your potholes and ultimately, because of that superpower, neuroplasticity, fill in those potholes.

KNOW WHERE YOUR
POTHOLES ARE

If Danya had known about the BGP, she could have anticipated situations that might cause activation and get herself grounded before the situation happened. Or, when she was caught off guard, she could have used the BGP skills to interrupt the very beginnings of reactivity. She could have used the last skill, Shift and Stay, before getting knocked out of her RZone.

When she got bumped all the way out of her RZone, stress chemicals blocked her ability to think clearly. That's when the fight, flight, or freeze responses take over. Which one of those three defensive responses did Danya get stuck in? If you believe she was in the fight response, you're correct.

FILLING THOSE POTHOLES

It usually takes practice before you can rewire your nervous system enough to respond in new, more constructive ways. If you use Grounding each night or every couple of nights at bedtime, you'll deepen your RZone because of neuroplasticity. And using Tracking during the day to stay in your RZone will help you avoid potholes of reactivity. Thanks to neuroplasticity, you can fill in your potholes rather than just avoid them, or worse, fall into them over and over.

This book's title refers to *Life's Heavy Lifting*. Some of the heaviest challenges in life are discussed in the next chapter. The focus is on traumatic experiences and how trauma affects the brain and nervous system.

Chapter 10

THE IMPACT OF TRAUMATIC EXPERIENCES ON THE BRAIN

"Life isn't about living a life without struggle. It's about living a life worth struggling for."

These wise words are from John Valverde, chief executive officer of YouthBuild USA, a nonprofit career initiative for young adults. Does anyone get through life without some struggle? There's a lot of "heavy lifting" in the lives of many of us. And some of those struggles rise to the level we call "trauma."

Traumatic experiences can make it very hard to live a life without struggling on a daily basis. The impact of those experiences affects the way the nervous system reacts to and processes daily experiences. Nightmares, pain, shutdown, sadness, and anxiety are just a few ways trauma gets embedded in the body. You might know people who've had traumatic experiences and have seen their struggles, or you may have experienced trauma yourself.

OUR EXPERIENCES SHAPE US

If you ever experienced or witnessed an extremely frightening event, you may have felt helpless, detached, numb, or volatile. You may have avoided a person or situation after a traumatic event because that person is a reminder of what happened.

Traumatic events can knock you out of your RZone, and the effects can last long after the event is over. You can't fully live the high-quality life worth struggling for if your brain is still wrapped up in and reacting to such an event as if it were still happening.

Our life experiences, both good and bad, shape who we are, and that especially includes the ways our brain and nervous system are affected. If you have experienced trauma, working regularly with a trained therapist can help. The BGP can play a supportive role in developing a self-care process that helps you live the life you want to live.

THE IMPORTANCE OF PROFESSIONAL HELP

If you have had traumatic experiences in childhood or adulthood, the best approach is to seek help from a mental health professional. This does not mean you are mentally ill. In fact, it is the opposite—you are aware that you aren't feeling like yourself. Getting professional help can get you back on track.

The BGP **is not a substitute for professional help**. Meeting regularly with a psychotherapist trained in treating survivors of traumatic events is a valuable and important step in regaining the life you want to live. The BGP can support you before, during, and after receiving professional help. You can use the BGP's five skills throughout the day to help you stay in the RZone. And when used before sleep or if sleep is interrupted by nightmares or fear, the skills can help you shift your attention to a resource that can build parasympathetic (calming) sensations in your body.

The BGP is a great supportive self-care practice to deepen your RZone so you can better deal with everyday struggles.

WHAT CLASSIFIES AN EVENT AS TRAUMATIC?

Trauma is more than simply unpleasant or painful—it is generated by an event that makes a very significant physical or emotional impact. The following events are considered traumatic:

- Natural disasters, like a hurricane, fire, tornado, flood, or earthquake
- Vehicle crash
- Shooting
- Robbery
- Domestic violence
- War experiences
- Immigration experiences
- Assault, including rape
- Childhood sexual abuse
- Childhood neglect, such as inadequate food, clothing, or affection
- Incarceration, particularly solitary confinement
- Oppression caused by systemic racism and other forms of oppression or discrimination (referred to as a "collective trauma")

You may have other events to add as well. Trauma can be the result of an event in which you are the victim—it happened directly to you—or it can be something you witnessed, sometimes called "secondary trauma" or "witnessing." Whichever form and whatever the cause, the severity of your brain-body reactions lets you know it was traumatic for you.

REACTIONS TO TRAUMATIC EVENTS CAN DIFFER

People react to the same traumatic events in different ways. Reactions can differ depending on various factors: how deep your RZone is, the quality of care and support you receive from others, previous exposure to frightening events, access to professional help, your degree of social and economic stability, and your age when the trauma happens (children tend to have longer-lasting symptoms than adults). Feeling helpless to get away from the event or blaming yourself for the event can add to its negative impact.

Earlier in the book, we explored the defensive responses of fight, flight, and freeze. They are triggered automatically as traumatic defenses. They aren't under your conscious control. Many of us have a default defensive response based on bad experiences in childhood. Some people's default defensive response sends them into fight and aggression, others freeze and just feel numb inside, while some default to the flight response and avoid anything that brings the traumatic event, including some situations and certain people. Do you have a default response when something frightening happens or when you are triggered by a frightening event?

USING THE BGP

This chapter focuses on how you can use the BGP in your daily life if you are dealing with the effects of trauma. It is important to emphasize again that **the BGP is not a substitute for psychotherapy**. It is a good auxiliary tool to help you deal with daily stressors as you go through therapy. You can also use the same BGP skills when you get bumped out of the RZone by something that isn't a traumatic event but is, nevertheless, challenging for you in a more temporary way.

Many good books on trauma give useful details that we won't go into here. Googling "trauma" online brings a variety of links to explore, and I encourage you to look through some trauma-focused books in a bookstore or online to see which seem most relevant to you. Books that include worksheets can be especially helpful in addressing information about your symptoms, coping strategies, and the differences between stress, distress, and posttraumatic stress disorder (PTSD), a term used to describe the negative, long-term consequences of a traumatic event.

THE ROLE OF THE AMYGDALA

Remember that structure in your brain, the amygdala, your brain's smoke detector? It's the fingernail in Siegel's hand brain model, and it can get wildly miscalibrated when you experience a traumatic event. It's as if the amygdala becomes stuck on high alert, and it perceives everything as a threat. These are some of the ways the amygdala's high-alert signal shows up:

- **Physical signs**: pain, trouble breathing, dizziness, fatigue, heart pounding or racing, high blood pressure, nausea, and sleep problems, including nightmares
- **Emotional signs**: fear, depression, hopelessness, feeling helpless, denial, volatility, anger, mood swings, sadness, grief, overwhelm, loss of faith, or feeling suicidal (the National Suicide Hotline is 1-800-273-8255 and has people on the phones twenty-four hours a day)

- **Cognitive signs**: blaming others, confusion, trouble making decisions, concentration problems, distorted thinking, and negative self-talk
- **Behavioral signs**: emotional outbursts, social withdrawal, aggressive behaviors, or risky behaviors such as gambling, buying sprees, promiscuity, loss of faith, avoidance, and misuse of substances (drugs, alcohol, food) to numb out

You may experience some symptoms from every category, or your symptoms may be primarily from one category. You can see how profoundly a traumatic event can impact your life. It can even result in the alienation of the people who care most about you.

UNDIGESTED TRAUMA

When the effects of a frightening experience don't fade away, I call it "undigested trauma." It means your brain-body system has not fully recovered from the event, and it often seems as if the event is still happening. Undigested trauma can sap the joy out of life. And negative sensory triggers make the trauma seem as if it's happening again, and again, and again.

Negative triggers can be a big part of living with undigested trauma. The smells, sights, sounds, and types of touch that were part of the traumatic event can set off strong reactions of fear, anger, and sadness months and even years after the traumatic event has been over. It feels as if the trauma is happening all over again. Please seek professional help if you experience these negative triggers.

THE KEY TO RESILIENCE AFTER TRAUMA

There is always the potential for hope and growth after trauma, and one important key—a superpower—is controlling your attention. The BGP's skills are all attention-based. Each skill helps you recalibrate that smoke detector in your brain, the amygdala. The amygdala sends your attention to the negative, to what is unexpected in your environment that might be a threat—even when it isn't. Learning to shift your attention and settle your nervous system reactivity makes a big difference in how you experience your life.

Here's an example of how Jeff used BGP while he was in psychotherapy for a traumatic event that he had experienced ten years before he entered therapy. The undigested trauma caused him to be reactive with his wife, and it was harming their relationship. The therapist was working with Jeff, who was learning to express his feelings better, to share them with his wife, to ask her for what he needed, and to hear what she needed from him.

At home, Jeff used his BGP skills in several ways. First, he became very good at Tracking sensations in his body, particularly sensations that indicated rising reactivity. He also used BGP skills as soon as he noticed the rising sympathetic activation—either Grounding or Resourcing to build a sense of calming. He preferred to use Grounding when he was with his wife. He shifted his attention to the support of the floor under his feet. His wife wouldn't even have to know he was doing it.

He would shift his attention away from the tension between them to the solid wooden floor and keep his attention focused on that stable support until his breathing deepened. Once he tracked deeper breathing returning, he knew he could continue the conversation with his wife. From inside his RZone, he could think more clearly and make better choices about how to handle whatever was causing the reactivity.

Jeff had sleep problems and sometimes woke in the night with nightmares. He used Resourcing and Resource strengthening when he went to bed as a way to get to sleep. His favorite resource image was being on a lake with his buddy fishing. He used Resource Strengthening to bring up all the smells (he actually loved the smell of fish), the sounds on the lake, and the conversations his friend and he would have. They often involved a lot of laughter and teasing. He began falling asleep more easily. And, he knew that if he woke in the night, he could take himself right back to the lake and sense into all those details of his resource until he relaxed enough to drift off to sleep again. He described feeling in control of his sleep in a way he had never felt before.

His wife noticed the difference in how Jeff handled tension at home. He told her about the BGP skills and showed her the Grounding and Resourcing scripts that are in the back of this book. Together they began using the BGP skills.

His therapist also noticed that he could better work with her during their therapy sessions. She told him he seemed to have an improved level of self-awareness.

Our brain-body system is wired for resilience. We all have the potential for it. And, by drawing on neuroplasticity, the brain's ability to change, you can do all of the following:

- Learn to pay attention to your level of calmness or reactivity.
- Deepen your RZone by practicing the five BGP skills.
- Use the skill of Tracking to notice when sensations in your body are calming, neutral, or activated, or to track when your attention is focused on anything negative that makes your reactivity level rise and stress chemicals surge.

- Interrupt your amygdala's negativity bias before it gears up to the level of fight, flight, or freeze. BGP skills like Shift and Stay can help.
- Use the BGP skills of Grounding, Resourcing, and Resource Strengthening to focus attention on positives that bring parasympathetic balance to your nervous system.
- Apply the skill of Shift and Stay to shift and keep your attention on something that brings a sense of calm.

The more you apply the program, the more stability you wire into your brain-body system. That's neuroplasticity working on your behalf! You don't have to wait until something spikes you out of your RZone. You can use the BGP skills of Grounding, Resourcing, Resource Strengthening, and Shift and Stay anytime as a self-care practice to create parasympathetic calming. Practice the skills wherever you are during the day since no one can tell you're using them. It's a lovely, healthful break that takes only a minute or two.

Chapter 11

PRACTICE MAKES THE PROCESS GROW STRONGER

For many years I had a psychotherapy practice in Washington, DC. I asked my clients, each time they arrived ready to talk about their challenges, to first tell me about one thing they noticed on the way to my office that brought just a little moment of joy, comfort, gratitude, or fun—any small sense of well-being—a resource. We would then strengthen the sensations of calm and well-being that arose.

At first, some clients resisted. They were so much better at directing their attention to the negatives, letting the amygdala run the show. But the more they practiced noticing small appreciations—a rose blooming, the warmth of the sun, a smile from a passerby—the easier it got. Thanks, neuroplasticity! It's an excellent superpower tool.

SENSORY TRACKING MAKES THE DIFFERENCE

Using the BGP skill of Tracking, my clients got better and better at paying attention to the calming of parasympathetic sensations as well as savoring and strengthening them. The ability to stay longer in the calming sensations was deepening their RZones. As weeks passed, many reported that they weren't getting rattled as often by stressors. You, too, can build this simple practice of noticing small pleasures in your day. And don't forget to track how your body responds. That's essential. Does your breathing get a little deeper and slower? Does muscle tension relax? What else does your body do to indicate greater calmness?

So often, those positive things happen, and we simply don't pay attention to them long enough to give the parasympathetic calming sensations the time to grow and expand in the body. However, if you take charge of your attention and keep it focused on all the little details of that positive moment— that's Resource Strengthening—you'll build a nervous system with a deeper RZone. You'll be creating a climate of health in your body. And, you're likely to enjoy your life more, too.

Simply paying attention to the pleasant little details overrides your amygdala's focus on what's negative or threatening. It is that easy, and it can change your life. Taking charge of your attention by using the BGP's neuroscience-based skills—it is truly a superpower tool kit!

JENINE'S STORY

The BGP's skills changed Jenine's life when she reentered her community after incarceration. She served eight years, and with each year, she became increasingly aggressive and reactive. She told me the very worst part of her time in prison was when she was put in solitary confinement. She said she did things in solitary she wouldn't want to tell anyone.

I met Jenine three months after her release, when she came to a BGP training workshop I was conducting at her workplace. She was determined to rebuild her life and wanted to be better able to "keep my cool." But as she talked to me about her postprison life, I heard in her voice and saw in her body language (I was Tracking her as she talked) that she was in distress. I could tell by the speed at which she talked, the way she kept shifting in her chair, and how her eyes flitted around the room.

I described what I was noticing and expressed my concern for her. Jenine began to cry. She said, "It's been so long since anyone has paid attention to me in a good way." As she talked, she tensed up even more. Her jaw clenched. She was scowling. She told me that something had been happening to her regularly since she'd gotten out of prison, and it was causing her embarrassment and fear.

CELL CHECKS AND JINGLING KEYS

"What's happening, Jenine?" I asked. Her story poured out. When she was incarcerated, cell checks were done at night. When Jenine heard the keys jingling as the correctional officer came down the row, her heart pounded, her mouth got dry, and she bolted upright in her bed. She wanted to hide under her bed, but she couldn't fit under it. She put her fingers in her ears, but it hardly helped. Eventually, Jenine could relax only when the guard was far enough away that she couldn't hear the keys anymore.

Now that Jenine was out of prison, the sound of keys jingling remained a negative trigger for her. When she heard anyone's keys (car keys, house keys) making a sound, she spiked out of her RZone and got stuck on high. She described a pounding heart, dry mouth, and panic. It had gotten so bad that even the *anticipation* that she might hear jingling keys filled her body with tension. She stopped riding in any-one's car. She avoided parking lots. She did not even want to go outside. Her world became smaller and smaller because of this negative trigger.

USING BGP SKILLS TO REMOVE A TRAUMATIC TRIGGER

So, here's what we did to remove Jenine's traumatic trigger.

First, Jenine learned about her amygdala, her RZone, and the importance of learning to take charge of where your attention goes. Then we used the BGP skills, beginning with *Tracking* to help her get to know her body at a sensory level.

We started with resources in her life. As she described a resource, I would ask curiosity questions to keep her in the story long enough that the parasympathetic sensations would grow stronger. Then I'd tell her what I noticed (from my Tracking) as she talked. I noticed that she sat up a little straighter, and her face looked more relaxed. My noticing those sensory changes helped her notice them as well.

Then I showed Jenine how to use the *Grounding* skill to build calming parasympathetic sensations. She put her atten-tion on the support of the floor under her feet and noticed the solidness of the chair against her back. When she noticed the solidness, her breath deepened, and her shoulders dropped to a more relaxed position. Jenine was amazed that she could help her body settle down so easily! She was learning to take charge of where she directed her attention. She was harnessing her natural resilience. This was exciting! Mastering where your attention goes is a powerful tool for creating the person you want to be.

Since Jenine was able to notice calming sensations after Grounding, we moved on to ***Resourcing***. Smells are easy to start with, so I asked her about smells she enjoys. Positive smells are resources. They build parasympathetic sensations when we bring them to mind and stay with them by noticing all the details (Resource Strengthening).

When Jenine talked about walking along the beach and the smell of the salt water and seaweed, I used ***Resource Strengthening*** to ask curiosity questions about her experience at the beach. In order to build calming sensations, I asked these and other Resource Strengthening questions to emphasize positive details: "Do you have a favorite beach that you go to?" "What about it makes it your favorite?" "Do you like to have other people with you?" "Tell me what a favorite day at the beach looks like." "What's your favorite time of day to be at the beach?"

Each time she named a detail about the beach, I asked for another one until Jenine had been talking about this positive resource for a few minutes. Resource Strengthening is the

BGP skill that dials the amygdala's negativity focus way down by keeping attention focused on positives. Jenine's amygdala had been stuck on high alert from her traumatic experience in prison, and Resource Strengthening was shifting that by putting her in charge of her focus.

TRACKING WHEN USING RESOURCE STRENGTHENING

I was Tracking Jenine as she talked, and I saw her muscle tension diminish. Her shoulders dropped, and she shifted in her chair to a more relaxed position. Her breathing got slower and deeper, too. I knew from my Tracking of her that the parasympathetic part of her nervous system was operating. But did she notice it?

I asked Jenine to track any sensations she noticed inside her body as she talked. At first, she had trouble noticing any sensations—almost everyone has trouble at first. But she did say she felt "better." *Hooray!* She was able to notice a change for the better! I asked her to track where she noticed feeling better in her body. She said she mostly felt better in her stomach.

We ended the session by talking about how she could use the BGP skills to shift away from negative trauma sensations the minute her attention went to them. I encouraged her to *shift* her attention away from the scary stuff by using Resourcing, and then to use Resource Strengthening to *stay* with the images, smells, tastes, and sounds of being at her favorite beach. This is BGP's ***Shift and Stay*** skill.

Jenine made a list of other experiences and people in her life that she considers resources. She has learned how to stay focused on her positive resources until she is back in her RZone. How does she know when she is back in her RZone? She knows by Tracking herself. She watches for deeper breathing, decreased muscle tension, and decreased anxiety and fear.

PRACTICE PROMOTES STAYING POWER

The more Jenine uses the BGP's attention-based skills to shift her attention when she gets activated by fear, the deeper her RZone becomes because of her brain's superpower, neuroplasticity. What Jenine practices gets wired in.

A month after our last practice session, Jenine called me. She excitedly reported that she had gone out with a friend, and when the friend got her keys out, Jenine gave herself a quick reminder of the beach. Because she had been practicing this resource and strengthening it, her nervous system was primed to relax—and it did!

Often, we don't even realize when we're practicing a response—we're on autopilot. We aren't in charge of where the amygdala is sending our attention. Maybe a certain behavior has become a bad habit, like pessimism, angry outbursts, or negativity. The skill of Tracking, when used throughout the day, helps you notice when you are in a calm state or when you are veering into a negative habit (a thought, emotion, or behavior).

Tracking gets you out of autopilot. You can weaken that bad habit, and when you regularly interrupt it, you prune it away. Remember, neuroplasticity can wire positive habits in and prune bad habits away. To prune negative thoughts, feelings, and behaviors away, shift away from the bad habit as soon as you notice it and focus on something neutral around you or, even better, a resource. BGP skills, when practiced regularly, can build good habits that become wired in. The amygdala becomes properly calibrated, and your life begins to change for the better.

You can use the BGP for yourself and to help others—it is all about owning your power over your amygdala by managing where your attention goes.

It is also a wonderful self-care tool. You are the commander of your brain-body system. When you take charge of your attention, your life changes for the better.

TRUE STRENGTH

Chinese philosopher Lao Tzu said, "Conquering others takes force; conquering yourself is true strength." You have the neuroscience building blocks and skills in your tool kit to conquer your reactivity, cut off stress chemicals that poison your body, and create nourishing relationships with others. True strength!

In the next chapter, you'll learn how to feed your brain. It includes one of my favorite stories.

HEALTHY RELATIONSHIPS NOURISH YOUR BRAIN

Positive relationships and safety are two important dimensions of life that the BGP enhances. When I was learning neuroscience in graduate school, a professor told us, "Safety drives the bus." He meant that in order to function at our best, we have to feel safe, both physically and emotionally. Safety shapes our life experiences, and our life experiences shape our sense of safety.

The quality of our relationships plays a big role in whether we feel a sense of safety. Safe relationships are those in which we feel known and appreciated for who we are. They are an essential part of living a nourishing life.

When you make it a goal to live your life inside your RZone and know how to get back into it quickly when bounced out, you're better able to build the supportive relationships you deserve. With a deeper RZone, you have fewer stress chemicals in your body. Your temper is less likely to flare up. You're a better friend, family member, and team member at work and play. Good relationships are "food for the brain."

TEARY-EYED TOUGH GUY

I met Joseph when I conducted a training workshop for his work group. As we were going around the table, doing introductions, Joseph said he had been out of prison for four years and was proud to be working in his community. He told us he was a very bad guy as a teenager. He ran with a rough crew that took great pleasure in vandalizing property and threatening people.

One night Joseph and two friends were going to rob a convenience store. Joseph was driving the car, so he waited outside. He heard gunshots, then sirens, and all the teenagers, including Joseph, were arrested, convicted of robbery and attempted murder, and sent to prison.

The rest of Joseph's story didn't come out until we talked about the skill of Resourcing. I asked each group member to identify a resource. I wanted them to understand that a resource can be all kinds of things—pleasant people, a special place, a loved one, a satisfying job, a favorite food, even the smell of your morning coffee. A resource can be anything that brings pleasure or calmness when you bring it to mind.

When it was Joseph's turn to name his resource, we were all surprised to see a tear trickle down his face. None of us expected that from him since he seemed to have a tough-guy demeanor—someone who wouldn't show emotion. He certainly got everyone's attention! We all waited, completely focused on Joseph's story, eager to hear what resource could be so powerful it brought this tough guy to tears.

JOSEPH'S STORY

Joseph shared his story about a corrections officer on his prison block. One day the officer came up to Joseph and said, "I've been watching you, and you have something special. I'm going to get you a job in the prison garden." Garden jobs were highly coveted in prison, giving inmates a chance to get outside and plant and harvest food. This was a big deal. No one in Joseph's life had ever told him he had "something special." And no one had ever offered him a positive opportunity.

Having a relationship with someone who believed in him changed everything for Joseph. He started to feel differently about himself and his future. When he completed his prison sentence, he found a job working with youth who were troubled like he was as a teen. He became that positive voice in their lives, as the corrections officer had been for him.

I have worked in many prisons and jails and have never heard a story quite like Joseph's. The positive attention he received was a turning point for him. While in prison, he discovered that he loved gardening, and by the time I met him, he was enrolled in landscaping school at night and also creating flower arrangements for special occasions in his workplace and in his community. The entire time Joseph was talking to us, tears trickled down his face—and the faces of some of us, too.

CAN YOU RELATE?

The people you are in healthy relationships with and your positive experiences with them are so important to your health and well-being. That's why I call them "brain food" or "resources." Can you focus on a time when another person did something that made you feel special and really cared for? Or, if that seems challenging, just bring your attention to an experience with another person that was in some way positive for you.

- **Step 1**: Bring the person and a shared positive experience to mind. People you love or like are healthy resources when using the BGP skill of Resourcing.

- **Step 2**: Next, focus on all the details you admire about that person and how it is when you're together. How many details can you bring to mind? Try to bring up at least five—a funny facial expression, common interests, a sense of humor, shared activities, and a generous spirit. Shower your mind with happy memories. The more positive aspects you pay attention to, the more parasympathetic sensations you build inside your body. This is the skill of Resource Strengthening. You are creating a climate of health in your body.

- **Step 3**: Now, direct your attention to the sensations you feel inside your body. Does your breathing get deeper? Does muscle tension lessen? Use the skill of Tracking, noticing where in your body there are sensations of calm or relaxation. Sometimes people need to do Resourcing several times before the body learns to respond strongly enough for sensations to be tracked. Don't give up—you are training your attention to notice your brain and body working together. Training requires practice.

RELATIONSHIPS IN UTERO
SHAPE THE BRAIN AND NERVOUS SYSTEM

Humans have a social brain. Our earliest experience is that of growing inside another person. That's the fundamental reason relationship and safety can be considered brain food. Your brain began forming partly because of relationships and the climate those relationships created in the uterus. Babies before birth are in a close relationship not only with their mother but also with their outside environment. The developing brain and nervous system are shaped by positive and negative prenatal experiences.

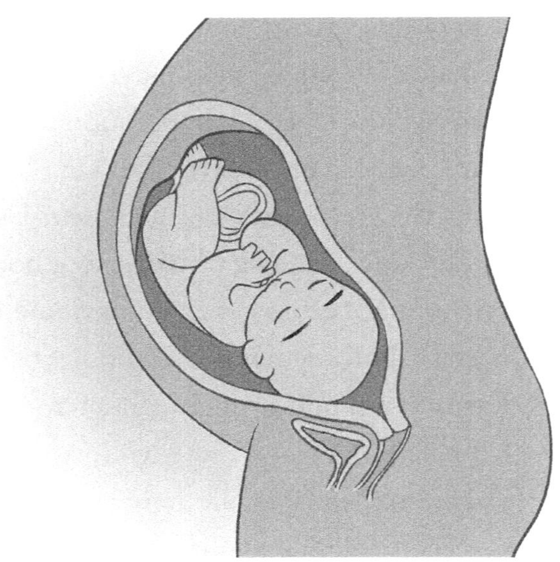

During your conception, there was never just you—it was you and the person you were growing inside of, your biological mother. And the intrauterine environment created for you to grow in was shaped, in part, by relationships in your birth mother's life.

What she ate affected you. The nourishment a pregnant woman takes in goes to the developing baby's brain. And, if, hopefully, enough nourishment is available, the rest goes to nourish the baby's developing organs. Food scarcity during pregnancy can affect organs as they develop in utero and can lead to health problems later in life.

By the second trimester, hearing is 100 percent developed. Imagine that. Even before birth, you could hear loud noises. You could hear music. You could hear the language that was being spoken. And, although you didn't understand that language, you heard the inflections and rhythm of speech from the outside world, and they became familiar to you.

Some pregnant women play soothing music during pregnancy to calm themselves and soothe the baby. Research finds that, after birth, that same music soothes the baby when it is fussy. The baby heard that music before birth and responds to that same music when it is played after birth.

Studies of developing babies, using a sonogram—a machine that can see the baby inside the mother—have shown that if a mother smokes during pregnancy, the baby recoils against the back of the uterine wall as if trying to get away from the smoke that comes through the umbilical cord. That's a flight response. That same recoil is seen in sonograms when a fight between people is happening with a lot of loud yelling. The developing baby can hear that stressful fight and tries to get away by recoiling. Pretty amazing, isn't it?

Prenatal experiences impact the way a baby's brain develops and the stability of its nervous system. Do you see how the quality of your attachments started long before your birth?

The quality of relationships throughout your life continues to influence your brain-body system. The BGP's neuroscience-based building blocks and skills focus on helping you create and maintain positive, safe attachments by helping you control reactivity and negativity.

Good relationships are healthy "brain food." As you use the BGP skills to decrease your reactivity and build resilience, you deepen your RZone. People with a deeper RZone can better withstand stressors and think strategically about what actions will best serve a situation. They are less exposed to toxic stress chemicals that harm mental and physical health. All of these factors contribute to creating and nourishing better relationships. Knowing we can help shape healthy brains in ourselves and our children by creating safe and nourishing relationships is beneficial. Brain food!

PRACTICE, PRACTICE...
AND PRACTICE

When you set a goal to live your life inside your RZone and know how to deepen that RZone and get back into it quickly when bounced out, you're better able to build supportive relationships and safety. The two go hand in hand. But it's not enough to know *how* to do it—you need to develop pathways in the brain that help stability and self-regulation become a regular part of your nervous system's functioning. That requires practice.

Practice is what enlists your neuroplasticity superpower. Anything you want to do well requires practice, including rewiring your brain. That's why I encourage you to use the skills as a self-care practice during the day or at bedtime—not only when a challenge arises.

Remember, the BGP skills, when practiced, deepen your RZone. You'll have fewer stress chemicals in your body. Your temper will be less likely to flare up. You'll be a better friend, family member, and team member at work and play. Safety and relationship—that's what it takes.

And, when you give your brain the healthy "food" it needs —healthy relationships and a nervous system that can manage stressors—you will be able to build a life that nourishes you and others.

NEXT STEPS

And, speaking of benefits, the next chapter is a Bonus Chapter. This is my special invitation for you to become a Resilience Messenger in your community. I invite you to share the BGP so others can learn to create emotional and physical health.

The neuroscience-based program you have learned here provides tools to help people harness their natural resilience. I invite you to join a cadre of Resilience Messengers who are sharing the BGP in their workplaces and communities. I provide a step-by-step guide for this wonderful tool, the BGP Skills Card, and I'm excited to show you exactly how to use it!

PASS IT ON! BE A RESILIENCE MESSENGER

Our world is full of challenges and controversy. Where do you stand? Partnerships provide a way of making a difference in responding to challenges in the communities that are important to you.

This Bonus Chapter invites you to share and spread the BGP's benefits community-wide. Will you partner with me and become a Resilience Messenger in your community by taking the BGP to others?

This is my special invitation for you. I invite you to teach people the BGP so they can create better lives for themselves. Teach them the science-based building blocks and the BGP skills that help regulate the brain-body system and decrease reactivity. Take the program into your community. The BGP skills put those essential neuroscience building blocks to good use.

The neuroscience building blocks provide a framework to understand what reactivity does to the brain and body, motivate practice of the BGP skills, and help each of us better understand reactivity in other people. The building blocks go hand in hand with the skills, making this a practical and effective program. BGP helps you and your community members create the selves each of you wants to be. Information is power!

I invite you to share the BGP to inspire others to create emotional and physical health. In this bonus chapter, I provide a step-by-step guide for how to use the BGP Skills Card with others. I'm excited to show you exactly how to use it!

LIFE IS ABOUT CREATING YOURSELF

For many years I have had a quote by the playwright George Bernard Shaw taped to the wall in front of my desk. The paper the quote is on is now yellowed and wrinkled, but its meaning remains relevant. It reads, "*Life isn't about finding yourself, it's about creating yourself.*"

Take a moment right now to bring to mind an image of the self you want to be. This is your Resource self. Pay attention to all the little details. Where are you in this image? How are you different—inside and out? Is there someone you want there with you? Put all the details into your image.

Now strengthen all of the resource sensations by noticing, or Tracking, every detail about this self you want to create. See yourself going through a day. Are you sleeping better in the image? Are you behaving differently? Are you accomplishing something you haven't been able to accomplish? What are you doing for fun and relaxation? This is the skill of Resource Strengthening. It's a resiliency booster.

As you bring all the details to mind, use Tracking to notice how your body responds. Put your attention on any parasympathetic sensations that begin to grow. Is your breath getting deeper? Is any muscle tension releasing? Where do you notice calming sensations in your body? Do positive thoughts and feelings arise? Let your attention drift around your body, Tracking any changes for the better.

After you have used BGP for yourself for a while, you might feel inspired to teach others the BGP. I've provided detailed explanations in this chapter for how to do that. As you create the person you want to be, you can show others.

They can then create changes they want to make. They'll learn to prune away behavior patterns that don't serve them. They'll also learn to pay attention to what they're grateful for in their lives. Of course, you must practice what you teach, so be sure to use the BGP in your own daily life!

As you use the BGP for your own self-care, some things that previously felt out of reach become more attainable. You will move toward new accomplishments, improve important relationships, and pay attention to the joy in your life—big or small. Maybe you will take on a project you have avoided. Or perhaps you will approach an important relationship in a whole new way. Imagine what that looks like. You're a pathfinder!

KEEP WALKING YOUR TALK

To be a Resilience Messenger, you need to walk the talk. I can't overemphasize how essential it is to consistently use the BGP skills for your own self-care before taking it into your community. Doesn't it make sense that you should regularly use the BGP for yourself if you want to be an effective Resilience Messenger for others? That way, you can share your personal experiences of building your new, healthier patterns of behavior and good habits via neuroplasticity. That way you become a credible messenger.

When you use the BGP skills, you discover, for example,

that at first, it can be hard to notice sensations in the body. The brain isn't used to paying attention at the sensory level—humans are much more used to paying attention to thoughts and feelings. But thoughts and feelings begin with sensations. When you learn to pay attention to and manage the sensations in your body, you can manage your thoughts and feelings rather than letting them manage you. You'll see for yourself the benefits that come when you stick to the practice—for example, recognizing that your RZone is getting deeper when you are able to avoid a heated argument by shifting away from reactivity. You can share these personal observations with your BGP Skills Card groups.

You can also share areas where you had some challenges applying the BGP. Maybe it took a while for you to notice parasympathetic sensations, or perhaps you didn't practice the BGP skills with consistency at first. Your firsthand experiences with the program help you relay to others what they might expect.

ARE YOU READY?

Ready to become a community changemaker? Ready to be a Resilience Messenger? The first part of the process is to give you some history about the special tool used to teach the BGP community-wide.

Second, you'll get a step-by-step method for using this tool—now called the BGP Skills Card—that I developed many years ago. It's been refined and adapted for use in many countries and communities. I make it easy for you to join me by giving you the BGP Skills Card. The card's development has a history.

IT STARTED IN HAITI

I was working in Haiti after the devastating earthquake of 2010. I went to Haiti every few months for two years, teaching traumatized people how the brain and body react to trauma—and how they could come back into balance.

Our team from the US offered a Train the Trainer Program (TTP) to a group of about twenty Haitian people who were living in a camp for displaced people. TTPs are important because the trainers become community messengers who help ensure the information lives on after our teams depart.

We worked in a lot of places without electricity. We couldn't use PowerPoint presentations that required a projector. Additionally, Haiti has a low literacy rate; there are some estimates that up to 70 percent of Haitians can't read well. We didn't want our TTP limited to only areas with electricity or high literacy rates. This meant we had to use training materials that didn't rely on a lot of words or technology.

One night I was lying on my cot, thinking about how to provide TTP to anyone. I've always liked to draw, just for fun. I took a pen and made little drawings illustrating what the skills look like. Take a look below, and you'll see my rendition of the skill of Grounding. Not very elegant, but it worked.

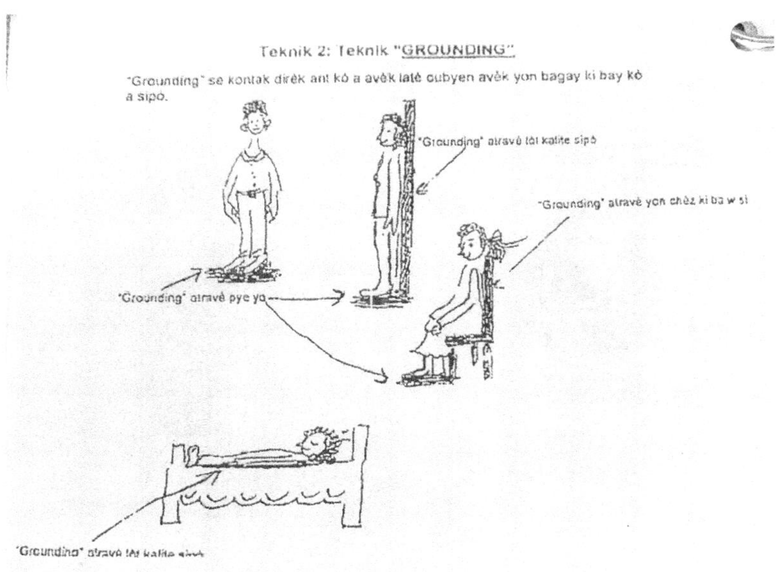

Our translators added a few words in Creole to describe the skill in each drawing, and we tried the cards out the next day. People were wildly enthusiastic! Now they had a way to remember details of the program and the ability to share it with others. The cards have evolved a lot since then.

The BGP Skills Cards have been invaluable to me for several reasons: Anyone can understand and use the cards. You have everything you need to teach the program to others. The cards are inexpensive to print. And people love having a tangible item to take away with them after a workshop. It helps them retain and practice what they've learned about the skills and how to apply them.

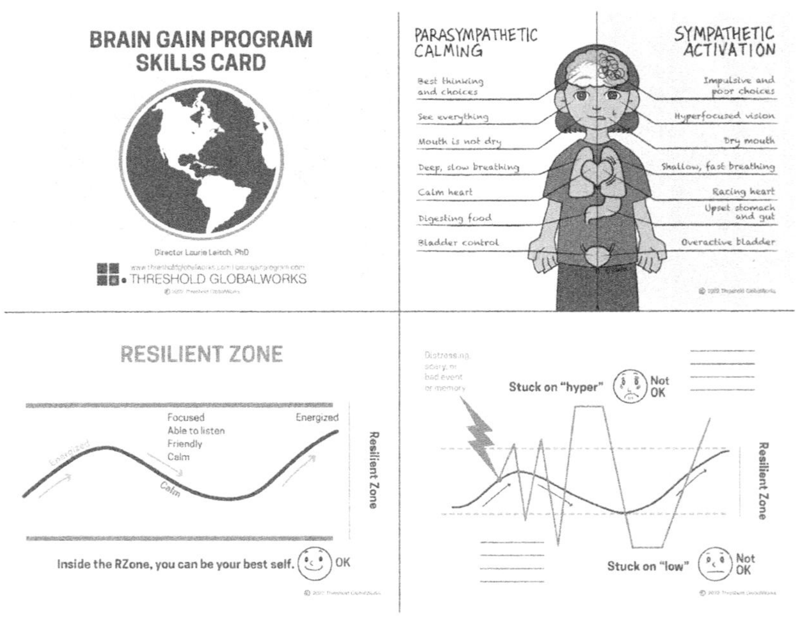

Side 1 Kids Card

While my hand-drawn cards were well received in Haiti, over the past twelve years, the BGP Skills Cards have been upgraded from those first simple drawings. Now each skills card is two-sided, with one side detailing neuroscience information and the other side demonstrating the skills.

Side 2 Kids Card

Except for those I drew in Haiti, illustrator Yoorina Seo has done the drawings for all of the BGP Skills Cards, of which there are now many versions. There is a skills card designed for people fleeing their country of origin to safety. A skills card for kids that uses simpler words and images (see above).

There are skills cards for residents of diverse communities. The cards that are specific to a country, like Nepal and Ukraine, have symbols and clothing styles typical of those regions. Another card has race- and gender-neutral images, so it can apply to any population (see below). Several BGP Skills Cards are in the back of this book for you to choose which suits you the best.

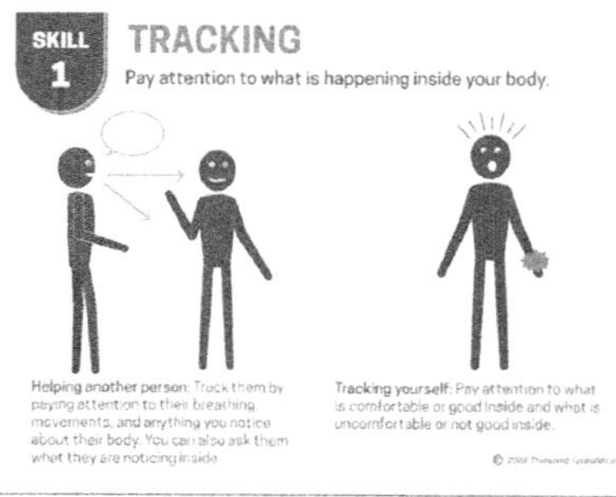

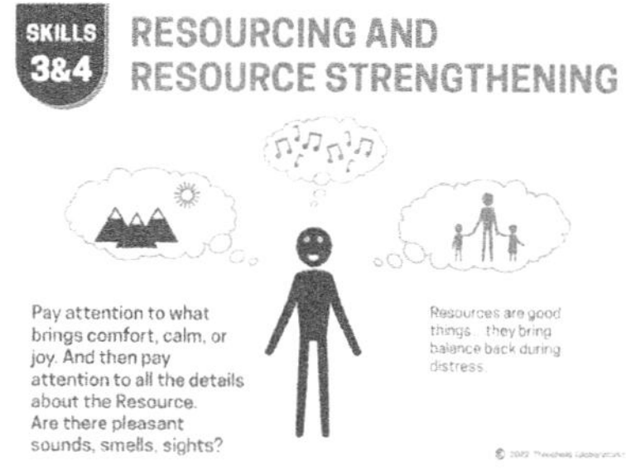

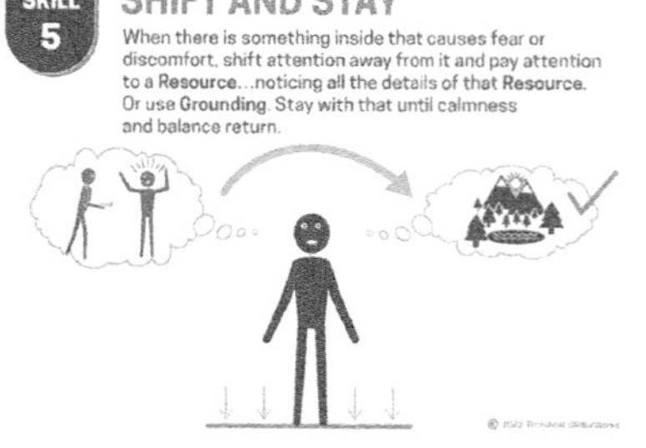

A TURNING POINT

Have you ever had a regular person become a teacher for you? Someone not educated as a teacher but who told you something you needed to know that made a big difference? I had an experience like that with the BGP Skills Card. It wasn't necessarily an easy experience, but it was exactly what I needed.

I wanted to use the BGP with youth who were in gang-related trouble in New York City. Before training started, I wanted to get opinions about the neutral skills card I would be using. A staff member of an organization I've worked with a lot arranged for me to meet with a group of four members of a crew.

They were sitting at a table in a conference room. As I walked down the hall to the room, I heard them laughing and talking with my staff member. When I came in, the crew members looked startled and suspicious. My staff member laughed at their reaction and said, "Yeah, she's white, but she's okay." That was all they needed to hear. They sat up and waited for me to explain the help that I needed from them.

I told them a bit about the BGP and what it does for the brain and body. I described how it's taught using the BGP Skills Card. I proudly put the neutral skills card on the table. I say "proudly" because the card shows stylized bodies filled in with black ink—no gender, no clothing, no bodily features, and no racial or ethnic characteristics. I was proud of the card because it can go anywhere with me—to other countries, to any kind of group. Here's what the neutral card's Grounding skill looks like:

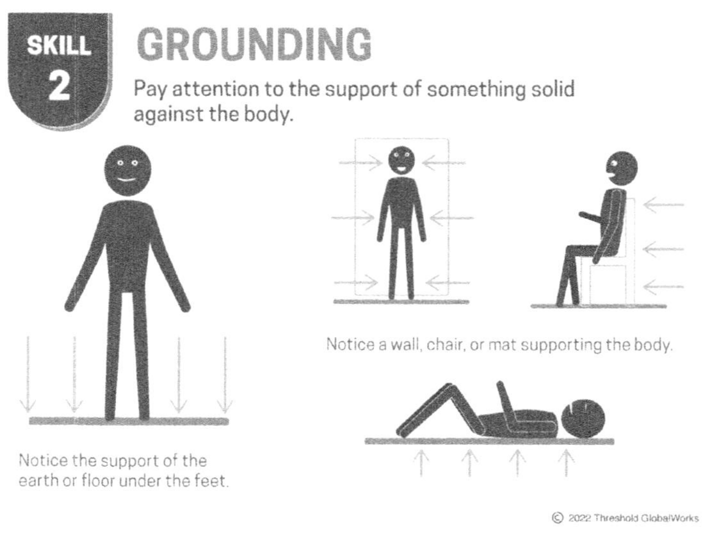

What I was most proud of, the card's neutral figures, were exactly what these guys didn't like. When I put the card on the table, one of the guys expressed disgust and batted the card away. Yes, he actually swatted the card down the table.

He told me he didn't like that the bodies were black but didn't look like black people. And there were other things he and the others didn't like about the card. For example, they thought the person lying on the floor (in the box that shows that Grounding can be done lying on a solid surface) had been shot. This was a good lesson for me. Just because a neutral card made my life easier by not having to make a new version for any group or country I was working with, it didn't necessarily resonate with everyone the way I had hoped it would.

I am so grateful for that blunt feedback. I went right to work. We now have many versions of the card, including one for people in diverse communities. I'm happy to say the card has passed inspection from people living in those communities. And, lots of people prefer to use the neutral card. See below for the Grounding skill on the diversity version of the card.

GROUNDING

Pay attention to the support of something solid against the body.

Notice the support of the earth or floor under the feet.

Notice a wall, chair, or mat supporting the body.

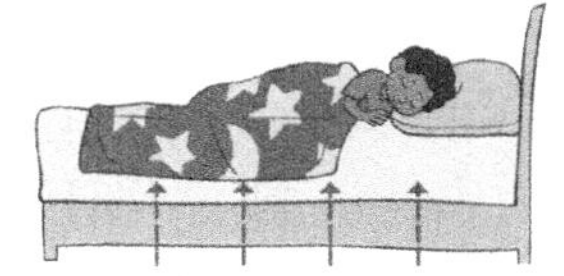

We have continued developing the card for the various specific groups we work with. We have a card for use with people in South and Central America who are trying to escape their country of origin to safety. Our Kids' Skills Card has slightly fewer and simpler words and includes a child using sign language and another in a wheelchair.

We have cards that are specific to a country—Nepal and Ukraine are examples. These country-specific cards have symbols and clothing styles typical of that culture. They are translated into the language of the countries each represents. You can choose from several BGP Skills Cards in the back of this book! See which ones you like best.

Now that you have a bit of the history of the cards, the rest of this bonus chapter shows you in a step-by-step way how to join me in the effort to spread this important information to others.

FIRST,
HAVE FUN WITH IT!

As you teach others to use the card, rule number one is to have fun by building relationships and a sense of safety. Those are "brain food" for a well-functioning group. For an icebreaker, one teacher had the class write the name of the type of weather they were feeling like as the class began. Each student then went to the front of the "weather map" on a whiteboard and stuck their weather report on the map.

At the start of a BGP class, we often use what we call "grabbers." Grabbers are statements, stories, or questions that grab people's attention. A grabber is anything that gets people to sit up and listen. A colleague of mine says a grabber is something that "makes people's eyebrows go up." It heightens engagement in the group.

These questions and discussion starters about the human brain are just a few examples of grabbers:

- Raise your hand if you have ever gotten into trouble because of reactivity. What if I told you that you have the power to change your own brain to reduce reactivity?

- Do you know that 77 percent of people experience stress that affects their physical health, and 73 percent have stress that impacts their mental health? That's a serious problem! Today you'll learn something we can do about that.

- True or false? Your brain is fully formed by age eighteen. Answer: This is false. The brain produces new neurons and learns new things for as long as you live. This ability is called neuroplasticity. It's your brain's superpower!

- True or false? Brain size does not determine intelligence. Answer: This is true. Albert Einstein was a genius, and he had a smaller-than-average brain.
- Have you ever made a mess of a relationship because of your reactivity?
- Have you had a lifelong dream you simply couldn't make happen? Did you just give up? Or did you keep trying?
- Do you know your brain is 70 percent to 80 percent water? What other interesting facts do you know about the brain?
- Imagine a day in your future when someone makes you mad or hurts your feelings—and you don't get reactive. You don't allow stress chemicals to poison your body because you know what to do to handle it skillfully.
- Imagine for a moment you're in the best relationship you could possibly desire. What exactly makes it so good?

You might also share the story of what got you so interested in the BGP that you chose to be a Resilience Messenger. The brain loves stories.

Once you've grabbed the attention of the person or group, you're ready to engage them with information about the BGP Skills Card.

BGP SKILLS CARD:
SIDE 1

Each side of the card has four illustrated boxes. Side 1 offers some basic neuroscience information about the human nervous system. We'll go through each box featured on Side 1 and list what to teach concerning them. Here, I'm using the BGP Skills Card used in diverse communities in the United States. It's in your appendix.

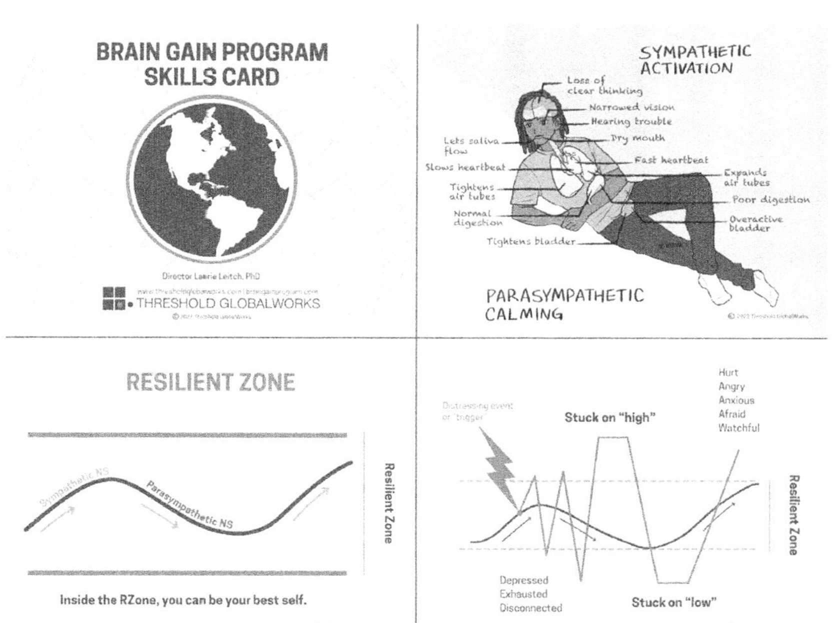

When presenting Box 1 with the globe of the world, introduce yourself, offer what you want to accomplish with the group, and share a little bit of how and why the BGP was developed. You can select information from earlier chapters based on what matters most to you and your group.

Ask group members to introduce themselves and to share what they hope to gain from the workshop. It can be fun to ask each person to share something special about themselves. This introductory portion not only helps you and members of your audience get acquainted but, just as importantly, it builds a sense of *safety* and *relationship* in the group. Remember, these two elements are food for a healthy brain.

Facts you can include in your introduction include the following:

- The Brain Gain Program was developed for use in communities, nationally and internationally, that have faced challenges that resulted in stress, distress, and trauma. It is also used for anyone wanting to build better relationships, reach for their dreams, and create a climate of health in the body.
- The Brain Gain Program is intended to provide science-based information and skills that build better emotional and physical health, decrease reactivity, cut off toxic stress chemicals, and strengthen resilience.
- Information is power. The Brain Gain Program is a tool kit. It gives you an easy-to-use set of skills that help you learn to take charge of yourself in ways that deepen what we call our RZone.

Box 2 on Side 1

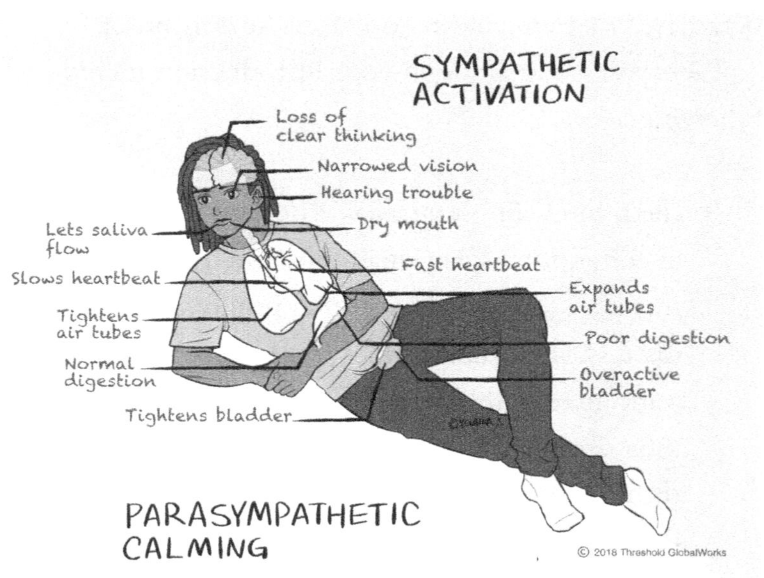

This box shows what the sympathetic, or activator, branch of the nervous system does when a stressor causes the release of toxic stress chemicals. The right side of the image illustrates how sympathetic activation affects various organs in the body. When I teach this box, I usually ask the group to raise their hands if the following questions are true for them:

- Have you or anyone in your family had asthma?

- Have you or anyone in your family had heart problems?
- Have you or anyone in your family had stomach or digestive problems?
- Have you or anyone in your family had cancer?

It is not unusual for most hands to go up in communities that have experienced trauma across generations (for example, due to racial and ethnic discrimination). This box shows the toxic effects of stress chemicals on the body's organs, which definitely gets people's attention.

Then, you shift to the left side of the body illustrated in Box 2. The left side of the body shows that the nervous system's parasympathetic branch does the opposite of the sympathetic branch. Parasympathetic responses slow the heartbeat, tighten air tubes in the lungs, and so on. They calm the nervous system.

That's a major reason the BGP skills teach the use of Tracking—to pinpoint signs of activation and calming in the body and show how to shift attention using the skills of Grounding, Resourcing, Resource Strengthening, and Shift and Stay. These skills build parasympathetic calming. That's the way to cut off those stress chemicals and keep a clear mind that can make good decisions and bring nervous system balance.

RESILIENT ZONE

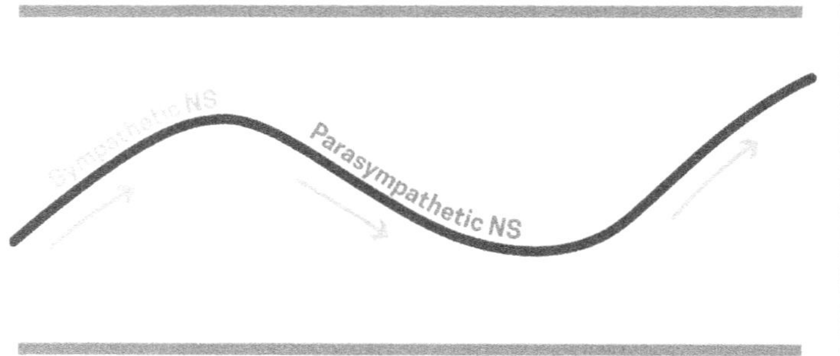

Inside the RZone you can be your best self

Box 3 illustrates the RZone you saw earlier—that important zone in our bodies that shows the rhythm between the nervous system's sympathetic and parasympathetic branches when there is a healthy balance. You can ask people their definition of "resilience" and then ask for some examples from their lives of when they were resilient. You can include the following when teaching Box 3:

- Your RZone is the range of functioning where you can think most clearly and be your best self.
- If you get activated, stress chemicals start to flood your body. They can cause inflammatory processes

and immune system problems if they stay in your body any longer than twenty to thirty minutes before you get calmer. Using BGP skills decreases your reactivity and gets you into a calmer frame of mind.

- You can make decisions that better benefit you and others when you are inside your RZone.
- You can be sad or mad in the RZone, but as long as you stay inside the RZone, you are not at such an extreme level that stress chemicals build up to harmful levels and block clear thinking.
- When you get bumped outside of the RZone, your access to your cortex, the thinking part of your brain, is negatively affected by all of the stress chemicals and high emotions.
- Some people have a very shallow RZone in which the smallest occurrence can bounce them out. Others have deeper RZones, so it takes a major stressor to bounce them out. The good news is you can control your RZone's depth.

Next, you can ask people for examples of what being in the RZone is for them and what kinds of situations bounce them out. This kind of discussion is important in building the relational safety the brain needs, and it also gets you better acquainted with your group and helps you know if your group members understand the concepts of resilience and the RZone.

In reviewing Box 3, point out the natural rhythm between the nervous system's sympathetic and parasympathetic branches. That relationship is like other cycles in nature—day following night, phases of the moon, seasons of the year. Like other parts of nature, our bodies have cycles and rhythms.

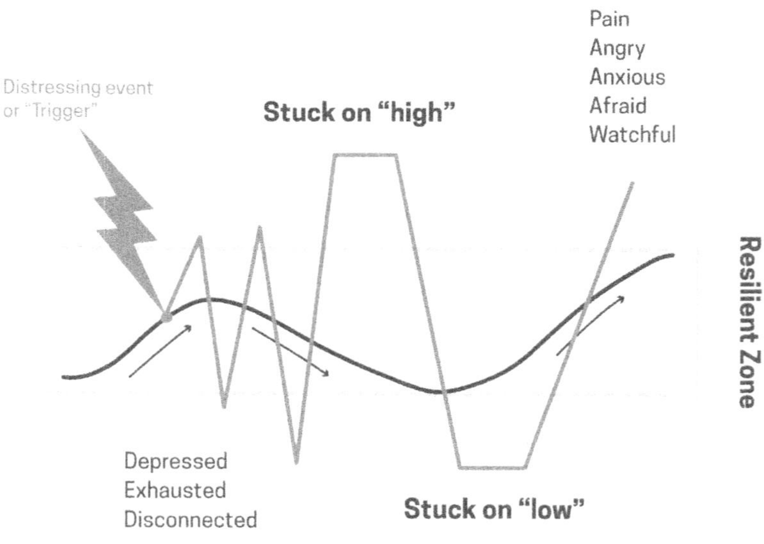

When the nervous system rhythm is in the RZone, things generally go well—internally and externally. But Box 4 demonstrates what happens to nervous system rhythm when that natural balance is disrupted by some kind of frightening experience. You can make the following points when presenting this box:

- When something unexpected happens, your body's smoke detector, the amygdala, goes into high gear. Its strong need for safety is thrown out of balance, and it prepares your body to fight, flee, or freeze. When you get bumped out of the RZone, stress chemicals stay in your body longer and can create health and relationship problems.

- When you get spiked out of the RZone—either above the RZone, becoming stuck on high, or below the RZone, getting stuck on low—your body is flooded with stress chemicals to help you escape the danger by fighting or fleeing. With some people, the rhythm bounces between those two extremes. (Point out that the box also gives examples of emotions and sensations that happen when someone is stuck on high or low.) Ask group members for their own examples of getting bumped out of their RZone—when they get highly activated, do they: (1) fight—showing anger or even physically fighting, (2) flee—leaving a situation, disappearing by using substances like drugs or alcohol, or (3) freeze—go into numbness or shutdown?

- A sensory trigger might bounce you out of your RZone. Triggers live in your unconscious memory system as leftovers from distressing events. (You could share the story of the former incarcerated woman whose trigger was the sound of keys jingling. Or maybe you have a story of your own.)

- Most of us have a default response in which we get stuck on high or low. Have you noticed if you have a default response? Defaults usually come from the way we handled scary childhood situations we felt powerless to change.
(My default tends to be getting stuck on low when I'm triggered by something unexpected. I go into a kind of disconnect, a freeze response. Do you have a default response? Share yours with group members to encourage them to share theirs too.)

BGP SKILLS CARD:
SIDE 2

The skills on Side 2 of the BGP Skills Card are designed to help deepen the RZone and help you either avoid getting bounced out or quickly get back into the RZone when bounced out. Side 2 shows the five BGP skills, with Resourcing and Resource Strengthening sharing Box 4 because they are always used together. Here's what you should point out as you introduce Side 2:

- Side 2 gives you all the skills of the brain-changing BGP. Each of the five skills relies on controlling your attention in a particular way.
- The first skill on Side 2 of the skills card, Tracking, shown in Box 1 on Side 2 of the skills card, is used in conjunction with all of the other skills. If we don't know how to track, we don't know when our reactions could be harming us by producing stress chemicals and impaired thinking.

Box 1 on Side 2: The Skill of Tracking

TRACKING

Pay attention to what is happening inside your body.

Helping another person: Track them by paying attention to their breathing, movements, and anything you notice about their body. You can also ask them what they are noticing inside.

Tracking yourself: Pay attention to what is comfortable or good inside and what is uncomfortable or not good inside.

© 2018 Threshold GlobalWorks

It is helpful to have group members do this simple exercise using Tracking:

1. Invite the group to each sit with their arms wrapped around themselves. Demonstrate for them, but don't refer to the gesture as a hug.

2. Then ask them to apply some pressure, a light squeeze, and stay like that for a minute, noticing, or Tracking, the sensations of pressure, body temperature, or other physical responses.

3. Have them release their arms and then track any changes in bodily sensations, such as breathing and muscle tension.

4. Ask how many people found that the squeeze felt positive. How many found it neutral? How many found it negative?

It's interesting to see that what is positive for one person ("It felt like a hug") may be negative for another ("I felt trapped") or just neutral ("I didn't really notice anything"). What's important is to know there is no correct or incorrect answer. Any sensory experience noticed by Tracking is fine. The point is to learn to notice bodily sensations, which may differ in people. Sensations are the language of the nervous system. Sensations aren't right or wrong. They are simply the way the nervous system communicates.

Examples of Sensation Words

The BGP uses the skill of Tracking with its four other skills to see how the body is signaling distress or calming. Examples of sensation words can be found in the following pages. Knowing examples of the body's sensations and sharing the list with your group will help you become an expert at reading your own body and helping others pay attention to what they are noticing in their bodies.

Although it is more common for us to understand our emotions and thoughts, sensations are what is behind them—creating those thoughts and feelings. The question to ask yourself or others is, *What am I noticing at the sensation level that lets me know I am feeling sad, mad, glad, etc.?*

Or, if you have a negative or positive *thought*, you can ask yourself, *What sensations do I notice inside my body when I have this thought or feeling?*

Positive sensations include the following:

Relaxed muscles • Deeper breathing • Soft, steady heartbeat • Peacefulness • Calm • Warmth • Smoothness and ease • Energized feeling

Negative sensations include the following:

Congestion • Spasms • Quivering • Constricting • Electric feeling • Throbbing • Prickliness • Shivering

• Cold • Heaviness • Dullness • Achiness • Nausea
• Fluttery feeling • Buzzing

Additional negative sensations that can be associated with trauma include these:

Constricted breath • Blocked throat • Breathlessness
• Heaviness • Pain • Agitation • Dizziness • Blurry vision
• Faintness • Chills • Shuddering • Nausea

Sensations associated with the release of tension (usually a positive sign that the body is discharging blocked energy) include these:

Shaking • Tingling • Heat or warmth • Trembling • Burping
• Yawning

Tracking is used with the other four BGP skills because people need to learn to notice what is happening in their bodies in order to best decide what to do about what they are noticing. By focusing attention on what the Tracking reveals, a person can decide to strengthen positive sensations by staying with them or decrease negative sensations by shifting attention away from them.

Shifting attention away can be about focusing on a neutral place in the body or bringing to mind a resource and strengthening it. When reactivity decreases, clear thinking comes back, stress chemicals stop being produced, and better relationships are possible.

Box 2 on Side 2:
The Skill of Grounding

GROUNDING

Pay attention to the support of something solid against the body.

Notice the support of the earth or floor under the feet.

Notice a wall, chair, or mat supporting the body.

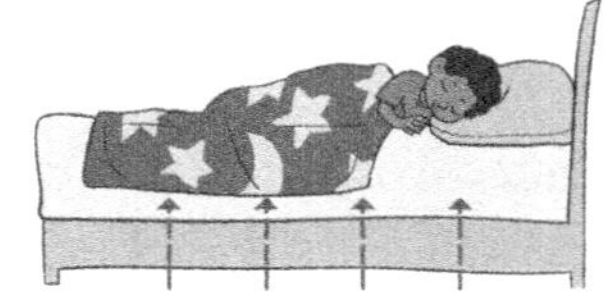

© 2018 Threshold GlobalWorks

You can include these points when you teach Grounding:

- Grounding is used in many traditions and is an ancient skill for bringing attention to the stability

of a solid surface against the body as a way of
generating parasympathetic sensations, which
are calming.

- Grounding can be done sitting down or lying on
the floor, on a bed, in the yard, or on the beach.
It can be done simply by pushing the palms of the
hands against a wall or on the surface of a desk.

- No one needs to know you're doing it, so you
can use Grounding in public when you notice
activation or reactivity beginning.

After detailing the above, you can use the Grounding
Script below to take the group members through Grounding,
reminding them to track the sensations that build as they
develop the skill. Ask each person to say one thing they
notice when using Grounding, especially listening for signs
of parasympathetic sensations: "I felt calmer," "I noticed my
muscles relaxing," "My palms stopped sweating."

Brain Gain Program: Grounding Script (For Use With Self or Others)

(Dots show where you pause. *It is important to pause* so the
sensations have a chance to build.)

When using Grounding for yourself. Read the script through a few times to understand the instructions and get them in your mind…and then put the script down and bring the instructions to mind and do each step. There is also a Grounding script in the appendix. You can make copies of it for group members to use.

When using Grounding with a group, read or say the script in a voice that is relaxed but not dreamy or slow, just at a regular pace.

1. "Just get into a comfortable position, in the chair, on the mat…or leaning against the wall."
2. "Let your eyes move around this space, just reminding yourself that you are right here, right now… You can do the rest of this with eyes open or closed, whichever feels best for you."
3. "Just let all of your attention focus down to the support of the floor supporting your feet… sensing into that support with all of your attention…"
4. "See what you notice inside as you do it…"
   a. "Notice your breath…Is it faster? Slower? About the same?…"
   b. "Notice your heart rate…Is it faster? Slower? About the same?…"

   c. "Notice any muscle tension…Is it more? Less? About the same?"

5. "Now just shift your attention to the support of the chair or wall against your back. Really put all of your attention there…and as you do that, see what you notice inside."

   a. "Again, notice your breath…Faster? Slower? About the same?…"

   b. "And notice your heart rate…Faster? Slower? About the same?…"

   c. "And any muscle tension…Is it more? Less? About the same?"

6. "Now start at the top of your head, and just let your attention drift slowly down, noticing any places in your body that are calm and relaxed."

7. "Then, gently open your eyes if they have been closed, and reorient yourself to the room or space."

If at any time during Grounding you notice a distracting thought or feeling or a little pain, just shift your attention away from it and put your attention on a place in the body that feels more relaxed, or at least neutral, and just stay there for a couple of moments.

- Then if you are using Grounding with another person or a group, ask the person or people in the group what they noticed inside the body as they went through the Grounding.
- Anything anyone noticed is acceptable, even if they say they didn't notice anything. It takes time and practice to learn how to pay attention at the sensory level.
- It is also essential not to judge anyone's report about what they noticed. Be accepting and curious.

Let people know it may take some practice to train their attention to notice sensations in the body. Because of neuroplasticity—the brain's ability to grow new neurons when we practice things—people can deepen their RZones. Be supportive of any sensations that members of the group report, whether positive, neutral, or negative.

Box 3 on Side 2: The Skills of Resourcing and Resource Strengthening

These two skills, Resourcing and Resource Strengthening, go hand in hand. Like Grounding, these skills are used to build parasympathetic (calming) sensations. These are a few factors to emphasize about Resourcing and Resource Strengthening:

- Because the amygdala, our brain's smoke detector, is so focused on potential threats, it takes diligence to help it break from its vigilance. Bringing to mind a positive resource is a good way to do that.

- A resource is anything that gives a sense of security, pleasure, or gratitude. It can be a person, animal, experience, place in nature, piece of music, your faith, favorite food or drink, and more. When you put your attention on a resource, it builds calming sensations—deeper breath, slower heart rate, decreased muscle tension, a sense of well-being.

- Resource Strengthening is an essential skill because it is necessary to maintain attention for a few minutes on a pleasant resource. Otherwise, the amygdala can sabotage your efforts to get calm.

- Focusing on at least four or five pleasing details strengthens the resource and builds those parasympathetic sensations, which are calming. Parasympathetic responses are like taking a resilience vitamin, which is very good for maintaining both mental and physical health.

A good group activity is to ask each person to share a positive resource and then have other group members ask curiosity questions about that resource to strengthen the calming sensations in the body.

Here's an example. Let's say your resource is your grandmother. Questions group members might ask to support Resource Strengthening could include the following:

- "What makes her a resource for you?"
- "What name do you call your grandmother?"
- "What is a favorite memory of her?"
- "Are there special things she has done for you?"
- "How do you feel when you're with her?"

Each of these questions encourages Resource Strengthening because it helps the person get immersed in the positive resource. That immersion builds the calming sensations.

Cautionary note: Sometimes, people bring to mind a resource of a person or pet who has died. They may begin to cry. When this happens, gently interrupt and sympathize with the loss, then ask them if it is possible to shift from the pain of the loss and stay with what makes that person or pet a positive resource for them. If they have trouble shifting to positives, suggest choosing a different resource so they can experience the parasympathetic sensations.

After asking Resource Strengthening questions, the next step is to ask the person to notice sensations inside the body while bringing any or all of the resource's details to mind:

- "What do you notice about the breath—shallower, deeper, about the same?"
- "What about muscle tension—is it more, less, about the same?"
- "What other responses do you notice in your body?"

These questions help train the attention to go where the person wants it to go—to something calming. Parasympathetic sensations will arise and get stronger as the resource is strengthened. Asking the questions as multiple choice (for example, asking, "Are the sensations more or less or about the same?") shows group members that any sensation they notice is acceptable. There is no right answer. It is their body's unique response.

Brain Gain Program: Resourcing and Resource Strengthening Script

Using Grounding, Resourcing, and Resource Strengthening with others helps people learn to notice positive, calming sensations in the body. Learning to access these parasympathetic sensations helps deepen the RZone and offers a way to shift away from reactivity that generates stress chemicals.

There is also a Resourcing Script in the appendix of the book.

When using this script with another person or a group, read the script in a calm voice—but not a dreamy voice. Be sure to pause where there are dots in the script. It takes some time for sensations to arise and then to be noticed, especially when people are first learning how to track sensations in the body.

This script can be used after you've used the Grounding script or as a separate way to:

1. learn to notice parasympathetic sensations,
2. decrease activation and bring calming sensations, and
3. deepen the RZone by practicing bringing calming sensations into the body.

Reminder: dots in the text below mean to *pause and track sensations in the body.*

1. "Most of us have things in our lives that bring a sense of joy, security, calmness… They can be places in nature, or people in your life now or who were important in your past. A resource can be a favorite pet, a special hobby, your faith, a favorite place to go, or even a favorite food. So, just let a resource come to mind now…"

2. "…And when you have it in mind, let it get stronger by noticing all the various details of that resource…Are there positive smells?…Sounds?… Where are you when you enjoy this resource?… Is there a season of the year, a temperature? Are you with someone, or are you by yourself?… The more sensory details you can bring to mind, the better…"

3. "And now, see where you notice the sensations inside as you sense into all the details about the resource…Notice your breath…Is it deeper, shallower, about the same?…Notice your heart beating…Is it beating faster, slower, about the same?…And, see if you notice any changes in muscle tension…Is it the same?…More?… Less? When you sense into the body, it is common to notice a distracting thought, a pain, or other less positive sensation. If that happens, just *shift* your attention away from that and go back to your resource, or to a place in the body that feels calm, and *stay* there."

If you are resourcing just one person, strengthen the resource sensations by asking at least three to four curiosity questions to strengthen the resource and hear their responses. These questions should be such that they keep the person focused on the details of the resource—not just a question requiring a "yes" or "no" answer.

These are examples of curiosity questions when someone's resource is a child:

- "What kinds of things do you best like to do with her?"
- "What is her name, and why is she a resource for you?"
- "Bring to mind a favorite time you have spent together, and notice all the details of that time."

As the person describes the resource, look for any signs of relaxation, peacefulness, or pleasure, and comment on them: "I notice as you just told me about her happy dance that you got a big smile on your face. What are you noticing?"

Then say, "Where do you notice the sensations inside as you sense into all the positive details about your resource?"

Box 4 on Side 2:
The Skill of Shift and Stay

SHIFT AND STAY

When there is something inside that causes fear or discomfort, shift attention away from it and pay attention to a **Resource**…noticing all the details of that **Resource**. Or use **Grounding**. Stay with that until calmness and balance return.

Shift and Stay, the fifth BGP skill, is a handy superpower skill in your tool kit. Here are some details you can include when teaching about the last box on the BGP Skills Card:

- The Shift and Stay skill is a reactivity zapper.
  It is a quick way to interrupt a spike of reactivity
  simply by first Tracking that you feel amped up

and, second, shifting your attention to the support of a solid surface by Grounding or by bringing a resource to mind and Strengthening it until the reactivity decreases.

- As with the other skills, no one needs to know you are using Shift and Stay. You don't have to close your eyes or change your position. You simply shift your attention to something that calms you and stay with it until you're in the RZone. You can tell you're in the RZone when your breathing isn't rapid, your heart isn't racing, and you have a sense of calm. You can also think clearly.

- Notice that all the skills in the BGP rely on your ability to notice, or track, what is happening in your body. Attention is the commander of your mind. The better you get at taking charge of where your attention goes, the better your life will be.

- When you track where your attention is, decide if it's useful or healthy for you. If it is positive, strengthen it, but if it is negative, shift away. You are creating the brain that will do its best for you. When you practice this in daily life, you are utiliz-ing an important superpower—neuroplasticity—to wire in a higher-functioning brain.

Once you have gone through all the boxes on the card, take some time for people to work in small groups together. On Side 1, one person introduces Box 1, another introduces Box 2, and so on. Then on Side 2, people can take turns leading the group in Grounding, as well as Resourcing and Resource Strengthening. The groups can come back together and describe their experiences.

Now, you have all the essentials for using the BGP Skills Cards to teach the BGP to family, coworkers, students, and other groups in your community. Three versions of the cards are at the back of the book for you to photocopy and use: the Neutral card, the Urban card, and the Kids' card. A list of sensation words and the Grounding and Resourcing scripts are also there. These can be copied and given to groups.

The website, **www.braingainproject.com**, is a place where you can ask questions, share successes, and connect with other Resilience Messengers.

CONCLUSION

That's What It's All About

"Give a man a fish,
and you feed him for a day.
Teach him to fish, and you feed him
for a lifetime."

—Lao Tzu, Chinese philosopher

As I've written these chapters, you've been on my mind. I've imagined the kinds of things you may have experienced in your life that got you interested in this book. I've wondered how you would respond to the information. Would you be excited at the prospect of taking charge of becoming your best self? Would you be skeptical at first?

I've pictured you using the skill of Tracking to spot reactivity as it begins in your body—then using the other skills to keep yourself in your RZone. My hope is that when you start to experience the difference this information and the skills can make in your life, you will excitedly share your success with others. At the very least, maybe others will say they are noticing positive differences in you.

I've felt excited to imagine you going out into your community as a Resilience Messenger for the BGP (if you choose to do that). As famed musician B.B. King once said, "The beautiful thing about learning is that no one can take it away from you."

Remember the story about how the residents of a camp for displaced people in Kenya banded together to buy the land the camp was on? This example of resilience should inspire hope, determination, and relationship. It highlights the power of shared purpose and community fellowship. As I write this, I can see the photo I took at that camp above my desk. A little girl, about five years old, is covered in dust but with a spirit that shines outward. With a big grin, hands on her hips, she's ready to help build a better life. Her parents have built a garden, and there are vegetables to eat!

As you use BGP for yourself, and if you take it into your community, just know that I'm here to support your efforts. I'd love to hear where and how you use the BGP for your own self-care. What changes do you notice? How often do you practice? What's the best result you have made happen for yourself?

And, if you take it to your community, tell me about your experiences. What went easily, and what challenges have you encountered? How did you deal with the challenges? I invite you to contact me with any questions and to share your experiences, results, and successes. My email is Leitch@ thresholdglobalworks.com.

And now, your BGP journey begins. I have a feeling that it's going to be an exciting journey! I end this book with much gratitude to you for joining me in the endeavor to build resilience worldwide. And, I am sensing into all the parasympathetic sensations that are growing as I stay with that gratitude! Such a blessing.

ACKNOWLEDGEMENTS

This book has been like taking a trip through the many projects, trainings, and countries that have shaped the Brain Gain Program (BGP), also called Social Resilience Model (SRM), over the past three decades. So many wonderful folks have informed my knowledge, teaching, and life over these years. I am grateful to be able to highlight them here.

Deepest gratitude goes to my wife, Loree; my kids, Chris and Lindsay; and my grandsons Nolan and Lucas. I count my blessings every single day for you!

Marianne Walters was an early influence on my orientation to resilience. Her focus on the competencies of single-parent families in the 1980s shifted attitudes from a lens of pathology to one of respect. Having had such a strong female mentor continues to shape my work.

Thank you, Angelo Bolea! Your fascinating class on neuroscience, more than twenty years ago, started me on an amazing journey that deepened my clinical work and inspired me to develop the work I am doing today. I am grateful to have experienced your creative strategies and enthusiasm for engaging the brain's amazing capacity in behalf of resilience.

To my stalwart clinical consultation group colleagues who, for many years, were essential in stimulating my work as a psychotherapist, thank you! Phyllis Jacobson-Kram, Halcy Bohen, Ruth Goldman, and Marty Gross, you contributed greatly to both my professional and personal growth.

I am very grateful to Peter Levine for being among the first to introduce me to the application of neuroscience to clinical work and for sending me to Thailand to use his model with highly traumatized people. Peter's Somatic Experiencing Skills are the foundation of my SRM skills. Through the Tsunami Response Project in Thailand, I saw directly how a neuroscience lens can be taken across cultures. Many thanks, Peter.

And, an acknowledgment also to Somatic Experiencing colleagues who inspired me to develop the Social Resilience Model (SRM), which now is also called Brain Gain Program (BGP).

Alexandra Merrill, you have been a stalwart and consistent influence on my development as a person and in my thinking. I deeply value your steady emphasis on the ways that racism, classism, ageism, and misogyny operate in our world, sometimes subtly and other times blatantly.

To Roshi Joan Halifax, a deep bow for your support of my work by including my teaching at Upaya Zen Center, most recently in the Chaplaincy Program. It is an honor to work with you and your dedicated students. Thank you.

For thirteen years I was a member of the Women's Leadership Collaborative. Thanks to each woman who opted into a learning community in which challenge and tenderness helped me learn so much about presence and accountability.

A big thanks to Ann Jacobs, executive director of John Jay College Institute for Justice and Opportunity. When I moved to New York City you opened so many doors to help me get started in a new, very large city. You supported my SRM (now also called Brain Gain Program) trainings and included my work in the Navigator Program, an amazing program for formerly incarcerated citizens. Thank you, thank you.

And, speaking of John Jay College's Navigator Program, an immense thank-you goes to the Navigator students. Over the five years that I have had the privilege of teaching each of you, I have been inspired by your determination, depth, and courage. I dedicate this book to you. May it contribute to healing in marginalized communities and in individuals who live daily with the impact of systemic racism.

Deep gratitude to the resilience-oriented administrators who have allowed my work to multiply through Train the Trainer projects in their states. Most recently, a special thank-you to Janice Lebel, director of the Massachusetts Department of Mental Health, and to Brittini Long, senior program coordinator-training division at Montgomery County Alcohol, Drug Addiction, and Mental Health Services (ADAMHS) in Dayton, Ohio. Each of you has an expansive and determined resiliency orientation to service delivery that led to over 110 SRM-trained trainers during a pandemic!

A huge burst of gratitude goes to all the Threshold GlobalWorks trainers who have contributed to high-quality training and have taken this practical model far and wide over these many years. Two deserving special mention are Kevin Barnes-Ceeney, University of New Haven, and Frantz Michel, founder of Dream Deferred. Thank you for all you continue to do with Threshold GlobalWorks!

This book is filled with fantastic drawings that illustrate essential parts of the material. They have been done by a talented graphic designer, Yoorina Seo. Yoorina has been endlessly patient as I made a multitude of requests, including designing the Brain Gain Program Skills Card images for use in Poland and Ukraine. Yoorina graduated from Arizona State University and currently is working as a graphic designer and illustrator. She lives in Texas. Explore more of her work at yseo8.myportfolio.com. Thank you, thank you, Yoorina!

APPENDIX

EXAMPLES OF SENSATION WORDS

The BGP uses the skill of Tracking with its four other skills to see how the body is signaling distress or calming. Examples of sensation words can be found in the following pages. Knowing examples of the body's sensations and sharing the list with your group will help you become an expert at reading your own body and helping others pay attention to what they are noticing in their bodies.

Although it is more common for us to understand our emotions and thoughts, sensations are what is behind them—creating those thoughts and feelings. The question to ask yourself or others is, *What am I noticing at the sensation level that lets me know I am feeling sad, mad, glad, etc.?*

Or, if you have a negative or positive *thought*, you can ask yourself, *What sensations do I notice inside my body when I have this thought or feeling?*

Positive sensations include the following:

Relaxed muscles • Deeper breathing • Soft, steady heartbeat • Peacefulness • Calm • Warmth • Smoothness and ease • Energized feeling

Negative sensations include the following:

Congestion • Spasms • Quivering • Constricting • Electric feeling • Throbbing • Prickliness • Shivering • Cold • Heaviness • Dullness • Achiness • Nausea • Fluttery feeling • Buzzing

Additional negative sensations that can be associated with trauma include these:

Constricted breath • Blocked throat • Breathlessness • Heaviness • Pain • Agitation • Dizziness • Blurry vision • Faintness • Chills • Shuddering • Nausea

Sensations associated with the release of tension (usually a positive sign that the body is discharging blocked energy) include these:

Shaking • Tingling • Heat or warmth • Trembling • Burping • Yawning

BRAIN GAIN PROGRAM: GROUNDING SCRIPT (FOR USE WITH SELF OR OTHERS)

(Dots show where you pause. *It is important to pause* so the sensations have a chance to build.)

When using Grounding for yourself. Read the script through a few times to understand the instructions and get them in your mind…and then put the script down and bring the instructions to mind and do each step. There is also a Grounding script in the appendix. You can make copies of it for group members to use.

When using Grounding with a group, read or say the script in a voice that is relaxed but not dreamy or slow, just at a regular pace.

1. "Just get into a comfortable position, in the chair, on the mat…or leaning against the wall."
2. "Let your eyes move around this space, just reminding yourself that you are right here, right now… You can do the rest of this with eyes open or closed, whichever feels best for you."
3. "Just let all of your attention focus down to the support of the floor supporting your feet…sensing into that support with all of your attention…"
4. "See what you notice inside as you do it…"

   a. "Notice your breath…Is it faster? Slower? About the same?…"

   b. "Notice your heart rate…Is it faster? Slower? About the same?…"

   c. "Notice any muscle tension…Is it more? Less? About the same?"

5. "Now just shift your attention to the support of the chair or wall against your back. Really put all of your attention there…and as you do that, see what you notice inside."

   a. "Again, notice your breath…Faster? Slower? About the same?…"

   b. "And notice your heart rate…Faster? Slower? About the same?…"

   c. "And any muscle tension…Is it more? Less? About the same?"

6. "Now start at the top of your head, and just let your attention drift slowly down, noticing any places in your body that are calm and relaxed."

7. "Then, gently open your eyes if they have been closed, and reorient yourself to the room or space."

If at any time during Grounding you notice a distracting thought or feeling or a little pain, just shift your attention away from it and put your attention on a place in the body that feels more relaxed, or at least neutral, and just stay there for a couple of moments.

- Then if you are using Grounding with another person or a group, ask the person or people in the group what they noticed inside the body as they went through the Grounding.
- Anything anyone noticed is acceptable, even if they say they didn't notice anything. It takes time and practice to learn how to pay attention at the sensory level.
- It is also essential not to judge anyone's report about what they noticed. Be accepting and curious.

BRAIN GAIN PROGRAM: RESOURCING AND RESOURCE STRENGTHENING SCRIPT

Using Grounding, Resourcing, and Resource Strengthening with others helps people learn to notice positive, calming sensations in the body. Learning to access these parasympathetic sensations helps deepen the RZone and offers a way to shift away from reactivity that generates stress chemicals.

There is also a Resourcing Script in the appendix of the book.

When using this script with another person or a group, read the script in a calm voice—but not a dreamy voice. Be sure to pause where there are dots in the script. It takes some time for sensations to arise and then to be noticed, especially when people are first learning how to track sensations in the body.

This script can be used after you've used the Grounding script or as a separate way to:

1. learn to notice parasympathetic sensations,
2. decrease activation and bring calming sensations, and
3. deepen the RZone by practicing bringing calming sensations into the body.

Reminder: dots in the text below mean to *pause and track sensations in the body.*

1. "Most of us have things in our lives that bring a sense of joy, security, calmness… They can be places in nature, or people in your life now or who were important in your past. A resource can be a favorite pet, a special hobby, your faith, a favorite place to go, or even a favorite food. So, just let a resource come to mind now…"

2. "…And when you have it in mind, let it get stronger by noticing all the various details of that resource… Are there positive smells?…Sounds?…Where are you when you enjoy this resource?…Is there a season of the year, a temperature? Are you with someone, or are you by yourself?…The more sensory details you can bring to mind, the better…"

3. "And now, see where you notice the sensations inside as you sense into all the details about the resource…Notice your breath…Is it deeper, shallower, about the same?…Notice your heart beating…Is it beating faster, slower, about the same?…And, see if you notice any changes in muscle tension…Is it the same?…More?…Less? When you sense into the body, it is common to notice a distracting thought, a pain, or other less positive sensation. If that happens, just *shift* your attention away from that and go back to your resource, or to a place in the body that feels calm, and *stay* there."

If you are resourcing just one person, strengthen the resource sensations by asking at least three to four curiosity questions to strengthen the resource and hear their responses. These questions should be such that they keep the person focused on the details of the resource—not just a question requiring a "yes" or "no" answer.

These are examples of curiosity questions when someone's resource is a child:

- "What kinds of things do you best like to do with her?"
- "What is her name, and why is she a resource for you?"
- "Bring to mind a favorite time you have spent together, and notice all the details of that time."

As the person describes the resource, look for any signs of relaxation, peacefulness, or pleasure, and comment on them: "I notice as you just told me about her happy dance that you got a big smile on your face. What are you noticing?"

Then say, "Where do you notice the sensations inside as you sense into all the positive details about your resource?"

An important note: Sometimes people choose a pet or a person as a resource who has died and when they bring that to mind, what they notice is sadness, and tears may come. If this happens, briefly sympathize with their loss, then ask if the person can shift to the positive parts of their memories and stay with those. If they can't shift to the positive, suggest they choose a resource that is all positive. Then ask curiosity questions to strengthen that alternative resource.

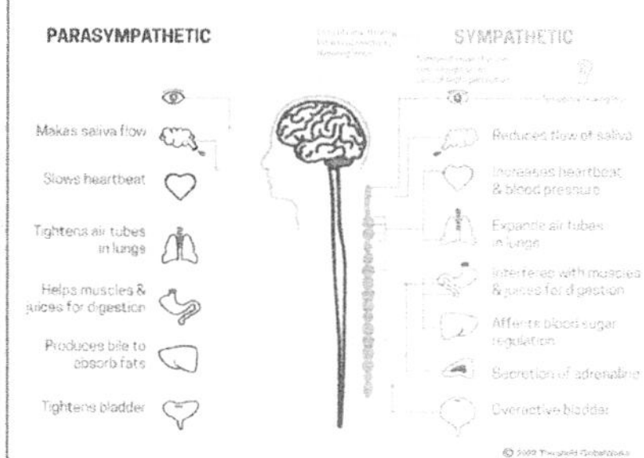

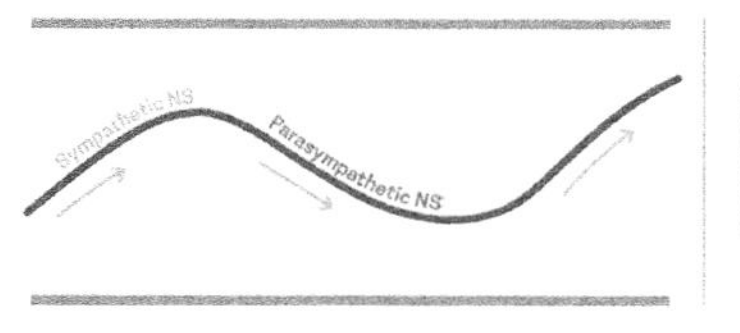

Inside the RZone, you can be your best self.

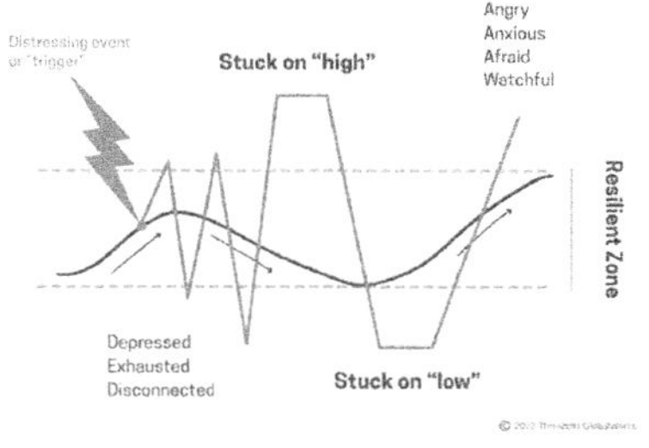

SKILL 1 — TRACKING

Pay attention to what is happening inside your body.

Helping another person: Track them by paying attention to their breathing, movements, and anything you notice about their body. You can also ask them what they are noticing inside.

Tracking yourself: Pay attention to what is comfortable or good inside and what is uncomfortable or not good inside.

© 2022 Therapist Collaborations

SKILL 2 — GROUNDING

Paying attention to the support of something solid against the body.

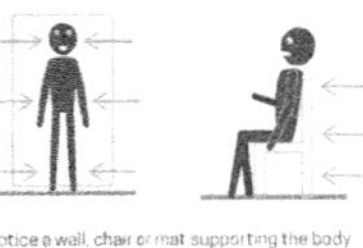

Notice the support of the earth or floor under the feet

© 2022 Therapist Collaborations

SKILLS 3&4 — RESOURCING AND RESOURCE STRENGTHENING

Pay attention to what brings comfort, calm, or joy. And then pay attention to all the details about the Resource. Are there pleasant sounds, smells, sights?

Resources are good things... they bring balance back during distress

© 2022 Therapist Collaborations

SKILL 5 — SHIFT AND STAY

When there is something inside that causes fear or discomfort, shift attention away from it and pay attention to a Resource...noticing all the details of that Resource. Or use Grounding. Stay with that until calmness and balance return.

© 2022 Therapist Collaborations

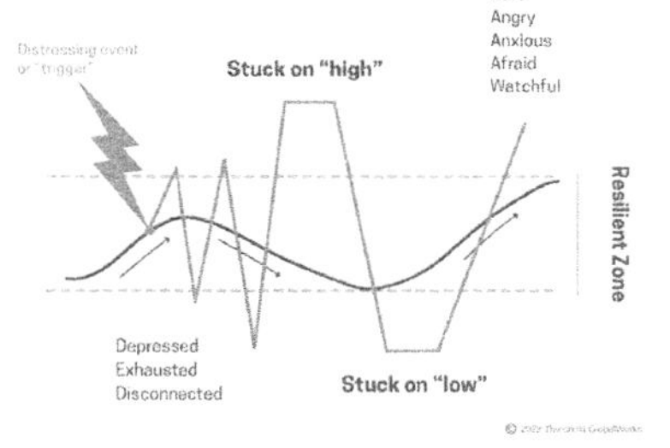

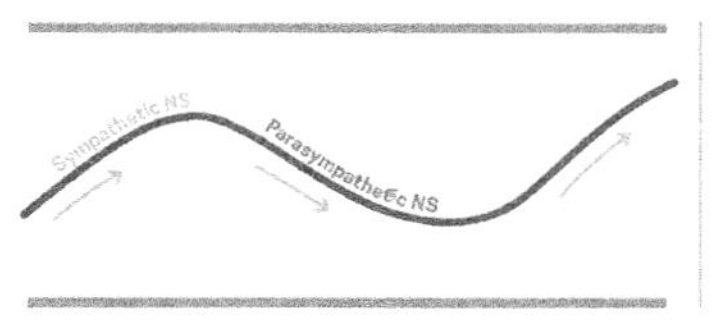

RESILIENT ZONE

Inside the RZone, you can be your best self.

TRACKING

Pay attention to what is happening inside your body.

Helping another person: Track them by paying attention to their breathing, movements, and anything you notice about their body. You can also ask them what they are noticing inside.

Tracking yourself: Pay attention to what is comfortable or good inside and what is uncomfortable or not good inside.

GROUNDING

Pay attention to the support of something solid against the body.

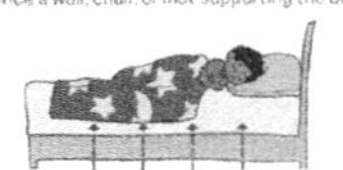

Notice the support of the earth or floor under the feet

RESOURCING AND RESOURCE STRENGTHENING

Pay attention to what brings comfort, calm, or joy. And then pay attention to all the details about the Resource. Are there pleasant sounds, smells, sights?

Resources are good things…they bring balance back during distress.

SHIFT AND STAY

When there is something inside that causes fear or discomfort, shift attention away from it and pay attention to a Resource…noticing all the details of that Resource. Or use Grounding. Stay with that until calmness and balance return.

BRAIN GAIN PROGRAM
SKILLS CARD

Director Laurie Leitch, PhD
THRESHOLD GLOBALWORKS

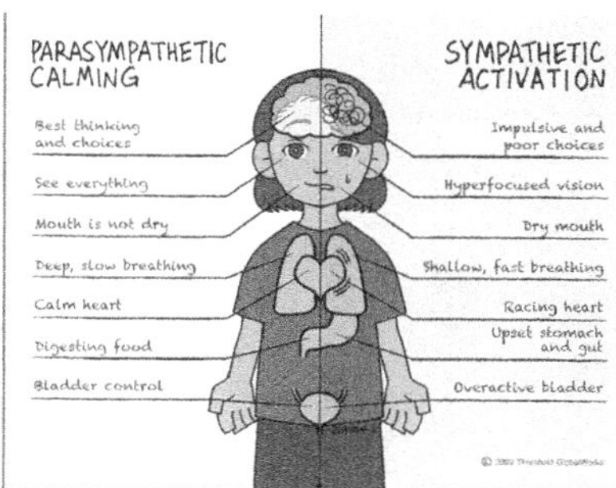

PARASYMPATHETIC CALMING
SYMPATHETIC ACTIVATION
Best thinking and choices
Impulsive and poor choices
See everything
Hyperfocused vision
Mouth is not dry
Dry mouth
Deep, slow breathing
Shallow, fast breathing
Calm heart
Racing heart
Digesting food
Upset stomach and gut
Bladder control
Overactive bladder

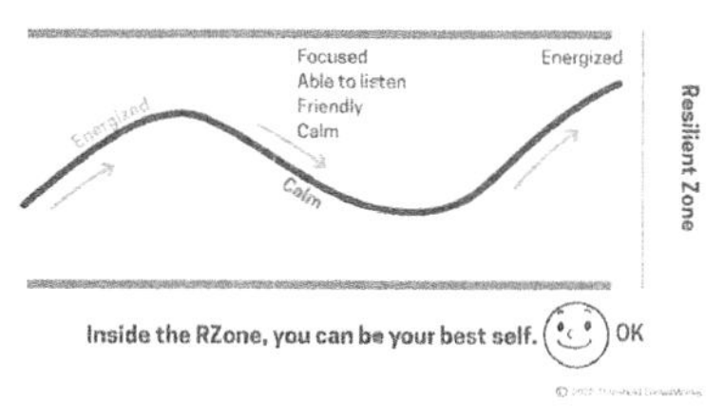

RESILIENT ZONE
Energized
Focused
Able to listen
Friendly
Calm
Calm
Energized
Resilient Zone
Inside the RZone, you can be your best self. OK

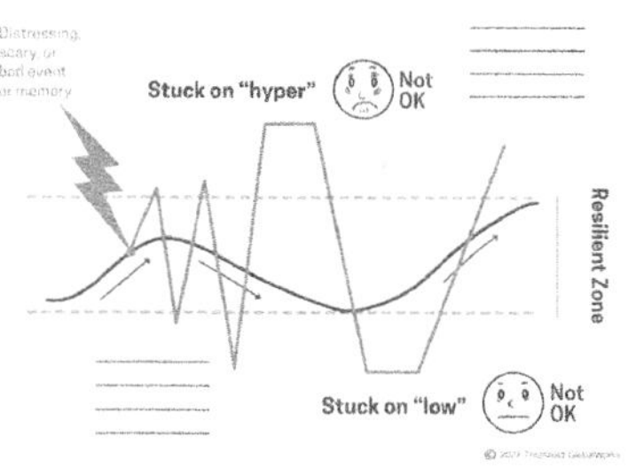

Distressing, scary, or bad event or memory
Stuck on "hyper"
Not OK
Resilient Zone
Stuck on "low"
Not OK

RZone SKILL 1 — TRACKING

Pay attention to what is happening inside your body.

Helping another person: Track them by paying attention to their breathing, movements, and anything you notice about their body. You can also ask them what they are noticing inside.

Tracking yourself: Pay attention to what is comfortable or good inside and what is uncomfortable or not good inside.

RZone SKILL 2 — GROUNDING

Pay attention to the support of something solid against the body.

Notice a wall, chair, or mat supporting the body.

Notice the support of a solid surface against your feet, arms, or back.

RZone SKILLS 3&4 — RESOURCING AND RESOURCE STRENGTHENING

Pay attention to what brings comfort, calm, or joy. And then pay attention to all the details about the Resource. Are there pleasant sounds, smells, sights?

Resources are good things…they bring balance back during hard times.

RZone SKILL 5 — SHIFT AND STAY

When there is something inside that causes fear or discomfort, shift attention away from it and pay attention to a Resource…noticing all the details of that Resource. Or use Grounding. Stay with that until calmness and balance return.

BIBLIOGRAPHY

BOOKS

Ayres, Jean A. *Sensory Integration and the Child: 25th Anniversary Edition.* Torrance, CA: Western Psychological Services, 2005.

Blakeslee, Sandra, and Matthew Blakeslee. *The Body Has a Mind of Its Own: How Body Maps in Your Brain Help You Do (Almost) Everything Better.* New York: Random House, 2007.

Bonomano, Dean. *Brain Bugs: How the Brain's Flaws Shape Our Lives.* New York: W. W. Norton & Company, 2011.

Cozolino, Louis. *The Neuroscience of Human Relationships: Attachment and the Developing Social Brain.* New York: W. W. Norton & Company, 2006.

Cozonlino, Louis. *The Neuroscience of Psychotherapy: Building and Rebuilding the Human Brain.* New York: W. W. Norton & Company, 2002.

Damasio, Antonio. *The Feeling of What Happens: Body and Emotion in the Making of Consciousness.* New York: Harvest Books, 1999.

Dennison, Paul, and Gail E. Dennison. *Brain Gym: Simple Activities for Whole Brain Learning.* Ventura, CA: Edu-Kinesthetics, Inc., 1986.

Doidge, Norman. *The Brain That Changes Itself: Stories of Personal Triumph from the Frontiers of Brain Science.* New York: Penguin Books, 2007.

Duckworth, Ken. *You Are Not Alone: The NAMI Guide to Navigating Mental Health—With Advice from Experts and Wisdom from Real People and Families.* New York: Zando, 2022.

Gendlin, Eugene T. *Focusing.* New York: Bantam Books, 1982.

Gilmartin, Kevin M. *Emotional Survival for Law Enforcement: A Guide for Officers and Their Families.* Tucson: E-S Press, 2002.

Goleman, Daniel. *Social Intelligence: The New Science of Human Relationships.* New York: Bantam Books, 2006.

Grossman, David, and Loren W. Christensen. *On Combat: The Psychology and Physiology of Deadly Conflict in War and in Peace.* Warrior Science Publications, 2008.

Grossman, David. *On Killing: The Psychological Cost of Learning to Kill in War and Society.* Revised Edition. New York: Back Bay Books/Little, Brown and Company, 2009.

Hall, Stephen S. *Wisdom: From Philosophy to Neuroscience.* New York: Alfred A. Knopf, 2010.

Hannaford, Carla. *Smart Moves: Why Learning Is Not All in Your Head.* Salt Lake City: Great River Books, 1995.

Hawn Foundation, The. *The MindUp Curriculums.* New York: Scholastic, Inc., 2011.

Herman, Judith. *Trauma and Recovery: The Aftermath of Violence—From Domestic Abuse to Political Terror.* New York: Basic Books, 1997.

Kagan, Richard. *Rebuilding Attachments with Traumatized Children: Healing from Losses, Violence, Abuse, and Neglect.* Binghamton, NY: The Haworth Maltreatment and Trauma Press, 2004.

Kahneman, Daniel. *Thinking, Fast and Slow.* New York: Farrar, Straus and Giroux, 2011.

Levine, Peter A., and Ann Frederick. *Waking the Tiger: Healing Trauma.* Berkeley: North Atlantic Books, 1997.

Loftus, Elizabeth, and Katherine Ketchum. *The Myth of Repressed Memory: False Memories and Allegations of Sexual Abuse.* New York: St. Martin's Griffin, 1996.

Loftus, Elizabeth, and Katherine Ketchum. *Witness for the Defense: The Accused, the Eyewitness and the Expert Who Puts Memory on Trial.* New York: St. Martin's Press, 1992.

Menakem, Resmaa. *My Grandmother's Hands: Racialized Trauma and the Pathway to Mending Our Hearts and Bodies.* Las Vegas: Central Recovery Press, 2017.

Newberg, Andrew, and Mark Robert Waldman. *How God Changes Your Brain: Breakthrough Findings from a Leading Neuroscientist.* New York: Ballantine Books, 2009.

Ogden, Pat, Kekuni Minton, and Claire Pain. *Trauma and the Body: A Sensorimotor Approach to Psychotherapy.* New York: W. W. Norton & Company, 2006.

Pinker, Steven. *The Better Angels of Our Nature: Why Violence Has Declined.* New York: Penguin Books, 2011.

Poole Heller, Diane, and Laurence S. Heller. *Crash Course: A Self-Healing Guide to Auto Accident Trauma and Recovery.* Berkeley: North Atlantic Books, 2011.

Ross, Gina. *Beyond the Trauma Vortex: The Media's Role in Healing Fear, Terror, and Violence.* Berkeley: North Atlantic Books, 2003.

Rothschild, Babette. *The Body Remembers: The Psychophysiology of Trauma and Trauma Treatment.* New York: W. W. Norton & Company, 2000.

Rothstein, Richard. *The Color of Law: A Forgotten History of How Our Government Segregated America.* New York: Liveright Publishing Corporation, 2017.

Sapolsky, Robert M. *Behave: The Biology of Humans at Our Best and Worst.* New York: Penguin Books, 2017.

Sapolsky, Robert M. *Why Zebras Don't Get Ulcers: An Updated Guide to Stress, Stress-related Diseases, and Coping.* New York: W. H. Freeman and Company, 1998.

Scaer, Robert. *The Body Bears the Burden: Trauma, Dissociation, and Disease.* Philadelphia: Hayworth Press, 2001.

Scaer, Robert. *The Trauma Spectrum: Hidden Wounds and Human Resiliency.* New York: W. W. Norton & Company, 2005.

Siegel, Daniel J. *The Developing Mind: How Relationships and the Brain Interact to Shape Who We Are.* New York: The Guilford Press, 2001.

Siegel, Daniel J. *The Mindful Brain: Reflection and Attunement in the Cultivation of Well-Being.* New York: W. W. Norton & Company, 2007.

Steinberg, Laurence. *Age of Opportunity: Lessons from the New Science of Adolescence.* New York: Houghton Mifflin Harcourt, 2014.

van der Kolk, Bessel A. *The Body Keeps the Score: Brain, Mind, and Body in the Healing of Trauma*. New York: Penguin Books, 2014.

van der Kolk, Bessel A., Alexander C. McFarlane, and Lars Weisaeth, eds. *Traumatic Stress: The Effects of Overwhelming Experience on Mind, Body, and Society*. New York: The Guilford Press, 1996.

Walker, Anne Graffam. *Handbook on Questioning Children: A Linguistic Perspective*. Chicago: ABA Center, 1999.

Whalen, Paul J., and Elizabeth A. Phelps, eds. *The Human Amygdala*. New York: The Guilford Press, 2009.

ARTICLES ON ATTENTIONAL PRACTICES AND IMMUNE FUNCTION

Davidson, Richard J., Jon Kabat-Zinn, Jessica Schumacher, Melissa Rosenkranz, Daniel Muller, Saki F. Santorelli, Ferris Urbanowski, Anne Harrington, Katherine Bonus, and John F. Sheridan. "Alterations in Brain and Immune Function Produced by Mindfulness Meditation." *Psychosomatic Medicine* 65, no. 4 (July 2003): 564–570. https://doi.org/10.1097/01.psy.0000077505.67574.e3.

Hein, Grit, and Tania Singer. "I Feel How You Feel but Not Always: The Empathic Brain and Its Modulation." *Current Opinion in Neurobiology* 18, no. 2 (April 2008): 153–158. https://doi.org/10.1016/j.conb.2008.07.012.

Jacobs, Tonya L., Elissa S. Epel, Jue Lin, Elizabeth H. Blackburn, Owen M. Wolkowitz, David A. Bridwell, Anthony P. Zanesco, et al. "Intensive Meditation Training, Immune Cell Telomerase

Activity, and Psychological Mediators." *Psychoneuroendocrinology* 36, no. 5 (June 2011): 664–681. https://doi.org/10.1016/j .psyneuen.2010.09.010.

Lazar, Sara W., Catherine Kerr, Rachel H. Wasserman, Jeremy R. Gray, Douglas N. Greve, Michael T. Treadway, Metta McGarvey, et al. "Meditation Experience Is Associated with Increased Cortical Thickness." *NeuroReport* 16, no. 17 (November 2005): 1893–1897. https://doi.org/10.1097%2F01.wnr.0000186598 .66243.19.

Lutz, Antoine, Heleen A. Slagter, John D. Dunne, and Richard J. Davidson. "Attention Regulation and Monitoring in Medita-tion." *Trends in Cognitive Science* 12, no. 4 (April 2008): 163–169. https://doi.org/10.1016/j.tics.2008.01.005.

Lutz, Antoine, Julie Brefczynski-Lewis, Tom Johnstone, and Richard J. Davidson. "Regulation of the Neural Circuitry of Emotion by Compassion Meditation: Effects of Meditative Expertise." *PLOS One* 3, no. 3 (March 2008): e1897. https://doi.org/10.1371 /journal.pone.0001897.

MacLean, Katherine A., Emilio Ferrer, Stephen R. Aichele, David A. Bridwell, Anthony P. Zanesco, Tonya L. Jacobs, Brandon G. King, et al. "Intensive Meditation Training Improves Perceptual Discrimination and Sustained Attention." *Psychological Science* 21, no. 6 (May 2010): 829–839. https://doi.org/10.1177/0956797 610371339.

Meeks, Thomas W., and Dilip V. Jeste. "Neurobiology of Wisdom: A Literature Overview." *Archives of General Psychiatry* 66, no. 4 (April 2009): 355–365. https://doi.org/10.1001%2 Farchgenpsychiatry.2009.8.

Pace, Thaddeus W. W., Lobsang Tenzin Negi, Daniel D. Adame, Steven P. Cole, Teresa I. Sivilli, Timothy D. Brown, Michael J. Issa, and Charles L. Raison. "Effect of Compassion Meditation on Neuroendocrine, Innate Immune and Behavioral Responses to Psychosocial Stress." *Psychoneuroendocrinology* 34, no. 1 (January 2009): 87–98. https://doi.org/10.1016/j.psyneuen.2008.08.011.

Singer, Tania, Ben Seymour, John O'Doherty, Holger Kaube, Raymond J. Dolan, and Chris D. Frith. "Empathy for Pain Involves the Affective but Not Sensory Components of Pain." *Science* 303, no. 5661 (February 2004): 1157–1162. https://doi.org/10.1126/science.1093535.

CLINICAL STUDIES
OF ATTENTIONAL PRACTICES

Carlson, Linda E., Michael Speca, Peter Faris, and Kamala D. Patel. "One Year Pre–Post Intervention Follow-Up of Psychological, Immune, Endocrine and Blood Pressure Outcomes of Mindfulness-Based Stress Reduction (MBSR) in Breast and Prostate Cancer Outpatients." *Brain, Behavior, and Immunity* 21, no. 8 (November 2007): 1038–1049. https://doi.org/10.1016/j.bbi.2007.04.002.

Carmody, James. "Evolving Conceptions of Mindfulness in Clinical Settings." *Journal of Cognitive Psychotherapy* 23, no. 3 (2009): 270–280. https://doi.org/10.1891/0889-8391.23.3.270.

Grossman, Paul, Ludger Niemann, Stefan Schmidt, and Harald Walach. "Mindfulness-Based Stress Reduction and Health Benefits: A Meta-Analysis." *Journal of Psychosomatic Research*

57, no. 1 (July 2004): 35–43. https://doi.org/10.1016/
S0022-3999(03)00573-7.

Krasner, Michael S., Ronald M. Epstein, Howard Beckman, Anthony
L. Suchman, Benjamin Chapman, Christopher J. Mooney, and
Timothy E. Quill. "Association of an Educational Program in
Mindful Communication With Burnout, Empathy, and Attitudes
Among Primary Care Physicians." *JAMA* 302, no. 12 (2009):
1284–1293. https://doi.org/10.1001/jama.2009.1384.

Reina, Michelle L., Dennis S. Reina, and Cynda Hylton Rushton.
"Trust: The Foundation for Team Collaboration and Healthy
Work Environments." *AACN Advanced Critical Care* 18,
no. 2 (2007): 103–108. https://doi.org/10.4037/15597768
-2007-2002.

Shapiro, Shauna L., Kirk Warren Brown, and Gina M. Biegel.
"Teaching Self-Care to Caregivers: Effects of Mindfulness-Based
Stress Reduction on the Mental Health of Therapists in
Training." *Training and Education in Professional Psychology* 1,
no. 2 (2007): 105–115. https://doi.org/10.1037/1931-3918
.1.2.105.

Teasdale, John D., Richard G. Moore, Hazel Hayhurst, Marie Pope,
Susan Williams, and Zindel V. Segal. "Metacognitive Awareness
and Prevention of Relapse in Depression: Empirical Evidence."
Journal of Consulting and Clinical Psychology 70, no. 2 (2002):
275–287. https://doi.org/10.1037//0022-006x.70.2.275.

RESOURCES ON STRUCTURAL AND SYSTEMIC INEQUALITY (MOSTLY U.S.-FOCUSED)

Alexander, Michelle. *The New Jim Crow: Mass Incarceration in the Age of Colorblindness.* New York: The New Press, 2010.

Brown, Dorothy A. *The Whiteness of Wealth: How the Tax System Impoverishes Black Americans—And How We Can Fix It.* New York: Crown, 2021.

DiAngelo, Robin. *White Fragility: Why It's So Hard for White People to Talk About Racism.* Boston: Beacon Press, 2018.

Hardy, Kenneth V., ed. *The Enduring, Invisible, and Ubiquitous Centrality of Whiteness.* New York: W. W. Norton & Company, 2022.

Menakem, Resmaa. *My Grandmother's Hands: Racialized Trauma and the Pathway to Mending Our Hearts and Bodies.* Las Vegas: Central Recovery Press, 2017.

Oluo, Ijeoma. *So You Want to Talk About Race.* New York: Seal Press, 2018.

Rothstein, Richard. *The Color of Law: A Forgotten History of How Our Government Segregated America.* New York: Liveright Publishing Corporation, 2017.

WEBSITES AND INTERNET LINKS

- Dana Foundation: www.dana.org. Many excellent articles and resources.

- Child Trauma Academy: www.childtrauma.org.

- David Baldwin's Trauma Information Pages: www.trauma-pages.com.

- HeartMath: www.heartmath.com.

- Keep Your Brain Alive: www.keepyourbrainalive.com. Includes exercises for stimulating the brain.

- Amen Clinics: www.amenclinic.com. Daniel Amen, ADHD specialist, website and information on changing the brain.

- NeuroLeadership Institute, David Scarf: www.neuroleadership.com.

Made in the USA
Monee, IL
07 July 2026